The COMPLETE POEMS *of*
MICHELANGELO

The COMPLETE POEMS *of*
MICHELANGELO

Translated by

JOHN FREDERICK NIMS

THE UNIVERSITY OF CHICAGO PRESS
Chicago & London

JOHN FREDERICK NIMS has published eight books of poetry, including *The Iron Pastoral; The Kiss: A Jambalaya; Zany in Denim; The Six-Cornered Snowflake;* and *Knowledge of the Evening,* which was nominated for a National Book Award. Among his previous translations are *Sappho to Valéry: Poems in Translation;* and *Poems of St. John of the Cross* (this last published by the University of Chicago Press). From 1978 to 1984, Mr. Nims was editor of *Poetry* magazine. He has taught poetry at a number of colleges and universities, including the University of Florida, Williams College, the University of Notre Dame, the University of Illinois, and Harvard University.

THE UNIVERSITY OF CHICAGO PRESS, CHICAGO 60637
THE UNIVERSITY OF CHICAGO PRESS, LTD., LONDON

© 1998 by The University of Chicago
All rights reserved. Published 1998

Printed in the United States of America

07 06 05 04 03 02 01 00   1 2 3 4 5

ISBN: 0-226-08033-1 (cloth)

Library of Congress Cataloging-in-Publication Data

Michelangelo Buonarroti, 1475–1564.
    [Poems, English]
    The complete poems of Michelangelo / translated by John Frederick
Nims.
        p.   cm.
    Includes bibliographical references.
    ISBN 0-226-08033-1 (alk. paper)
    I. Nims, John Frederick, 1913–   . II. Title.
PQ4815.B6A25   1998
851'.4—dc21

98-7704
CIP

♾ The paper used in this publication meets the minimum requirements of the American National Standard for Information Sciences—Permanence of Paper for Printed Library Materials, ANSI Z39.48-1992.

Contents

⮎ II ⮌
THREE LOVES (1532–1547)
36

ᥫ III ᥫ
THE FOUR LAST THINGS (1547-1564)
136

Preface

In the room the women come and go
Talking of Michelangelo.

THAT'S how T. S. Eliot, in his "love song" published in *Poetry* in 1914, characterized a social gathering early in the century. Some eighty years later I found myself at a party where again the name of Michelangelo was in the air. But very differently: gracefully at ease on a sofa by the fireplace, the women had settled into a discussion of an exhibition of Michelangelo drawings to be held at the Art Institute of Chicago in the spring of 1997. As staff members of the Art Institute, they knew what they were talking about. Drawn into their conversation, I ventured to ask if they were aware that Michelangelo had also written poetry.

How well, I wondered afterward, was his poetry known? How well did I know it myself? I had memories: there was hardly a day during the year we lived in Florence that I had not passed by or paused before something to remind me that more than half of his long life had been spent there.

Those memories touched on poetry as well as art. Beneath his bust of Brutus, the head turned haughtily away, was some scholar's elegiac couplet. The statues of the four *Slaves* in the Accademia delle Belle Arti, their agonized limbs straining to escape from the stone that imprisoned them, had once moved me to attempt a poem: a scribbled page from long ago had such fragments as "knee jutting up to jog its ankle free" and "the bent brow hammerlocked in its own arm."

Especially I remembered the quatrain Michelangelo had written for his languid figure of *Night* in the Medici Chapel, lines in protest of what he had come to see as the tyranny that had taken over the republican city of his youth. These are lines that one remembers without having memorized, translated, said Eugenio Montale, Italy's Nobel laureate, into every language in the world and affording the noblest conception of Michelangelo's sublimity.

It wasn't long afterward, in a *New Yorker* article on Florence, that I came across George Steiner's reference to Michelangelo's "polymorphic vision—a vision set out in opaque magnificence in his poems . . ." So the poetry qualified for words like "sublimity"? Like "magnificence"? This required looking into.

Checking on "Michelangelo Buonarroti" in a university library, I found more than I expected about the poetry: editions, translations, works of criticism. In what seemed the solidest of the studies, Robert J. Clement's 370-page *The Poetry of Michelangelo*, there was ample justification for the superlatives used by Montale and Steiner. His best poems, in Clement's estimation (341), "can be judged by any criteria whatsoever and remain at the pinnacle of Renaissance lyrical poetry."

So it seemed that de Tolnay's classic *Michelangelo: Sculptor, Painter, Architect* did not tell the whole story of this impassioned and tormented spirit, some of whose emotions and commitment neither sculpture nor painting was sufficient to convey. At a time when only a corrupt text was available, enough of its power had come through to attract such poets as Wordsworth, Longfellow, Emerson, and Santayana, each of whom had tried his hand at translating it. Wordsworth, after doing some of the sonnets, gave up in despair. As he wrote to a friend, Michelangelo's poetry was "the most difficult to construe I ever met with . . . I attempted at least 15 of his sonnets, but could not anywhere succeed." (At least a dozen of the lines he translated were not by Michelangelo at all, but by the meddling grandnephew who cobbled together the first edition of the poems.) In our own century, as great a poet as Rilke undertook the translation, but after working on the poems for several years he too gave up. E. M. Butler, his biographer and critic, thinks "Michelangelo was too great for him, too incomprehensibly great." Rilke himself, however, was pleased with the work he did complete, which was published in 1923. If we poor translators were deterred by awe, how much of the world's great literature would remain untranslated!

In more recent times, the best-known English rendering of the sonnets (about eighty of Michelangelo's some three hundred poems) has been that of John Addington Symonds, whose edition of 1878 was followed by many reprintings. Although a standard reference work says Symonds "excelled as a translator," readers today might balk at that opinion. Symonds favored a kind of poetic diction obsolete even in his day; he is fond of words like "fain," "aught," "nathless," "'neath" and "vauntful." In his translations we come across lines like

> the love of her
> but ill befits a heart all manly wise

and

> As thou wert erewhile wont my smile to bless . . .

This kind of diction, rarely heard from a living mouth, is not only factitious, but has a totally different effect on our ear today than Michelangelo's would have had on the Italian ear of his time. For the most part, for all its complexity of content, what he wrote was blunt, direct, plainspoken; in some of his poems (though not in the loftiest sonnets) there are even patches of the rough street-talk of his youth. The most famous description of his style was given by the burlesque poet Francesco Berni: comparing Michelangelo with other poets of the time, he says, " 'e dice cose, e voi dite parole,"—"he says things; you say words." Montale, himself the poet of rocky Liguria, goes so far as to say that Michelangelo, for his combination of ineffable thought and a technique rugged as stone, is un unicum forse di ogni tempo—unparalleled, perhaps throughout the ages.

As Glauco Cambon has said, Michelangelo's sometimes rough vocabulary "from the Arno's shore" was likely "to horrify the effete courtiers and Petrarchizing purists" of the time (7). It was hardly a language to be translated by "fain" and "nathless." Michelangelo spoke and wrote like the Florentine he was. Those who know standard Italian are surprised to come across spellings like "tucto" (for tutto) and "chome" (for come) in his work. Although Florence and Bologna are only about a third as far apart as Chicago and Detroit, the local accents were so different that we are told the Bolognese nobleman, in whose home Michelangelo spent a year, delighted in hearing his guest read poetry in his Tuscan accent. (Some of that accent must have lingered in the Florence we knew, particularly the aspirated c which turned casa into hasa, and which our young sons, who prattled in Italian, carried back to the Midwest when they munched on a piece of "handy" or watched a "howboy" movie.)

His combination of down-to-earth diction with his "ineffability" of thought and with his elaborate metrical forms has been a problem for many who have labored in what the art critic Waldemar Januszczak, in his witty *Sayonara, Michelangelo,* has called "the ugly annals of Michelangelo translation." I have not scrupled, now and then, to use such sturdy American words as "bogus" and "hog-tie," which some purists consider slang. The *New Shorter Oxford English Dictionary* is less hidebound; without disparaging either, it classifies the first as "Orig. *U.S.*" and the second as "*N. Amer.*"

Why, a month or so after the party at which there was talk of Michelangelo, did I find myself beginning to translate some of his sonnets? *Horror vacui?*—the void was there. I intended, at first, to do only a few, those that Clements and Cambon seemed to think the best. But when I had finished those few, the momentum carried me on through all eighty. Those done, there were the hundred or so madrigals, which showed another side of the poet's temperament. They came next. Then there remained another hundred poems in various meters—but it seemed too late to turn back. Like Macbeth, I had

> Stepped in so far that, should I wade no more,
> Returning were as tedious as go o'er.

What had kept me going, for a year or more, was the fun of it. "Fun" is a word that Robert Frost often used of poetry. If it offends anyone when used in the aura of the divine Michelangelo, as Vasari called him, we could retrieve from ancient Greece the favorite motto of Valéry, πρὸς χάριν, which he translates as *pour le plaisir.* I kept translating for the pleasure of it.

Not all translation is rich in the pleasure we call "fun." Word-for-word "literal" dictionary-scavenging can be dreary work, like a piece of assigned homework we resent having to do. The fun comes in when, by imposing obstacles, we introduce the element of sport or game, with its hurdles, wickets, sand traps, baselines, strike zones, bull's-eyes. So, in translating poetry, we have to cope with such tricky features as rhythm, sound, wordplay, connotation, and all the other enrichments that lift prose to a more resonant and allusive level. Incorporating as many of these features as the terrain allows is the goal of the translator: born of such fun is what we call fidelity.

The magnificence of Michelangelo's best poetry is by no means always opaque. But occasionally even those most qualified to interpret differ as to the meaning of this or that passage. As in the work of any important poet, there are the great poems and the ones not so great. Sometimes a poem fails because Michelangelo's phrasing is too compact, too cryptic for its meaning, sometimes because of what Cambon calls the "labyrinthine complexity" of its logic, in which the concept has struggled in vain to work free of its granitic verbiage. The occasional density has been a problem even for Italian readers, so that editors— ever since Guasti's edition of 1863—have provided poems with a paraphrase in everyday Italian. This is even more indispensable for the foreign reader and translator, less sensitive to nuance than the native speaker, who will have heard hundreds of times, in many contexts, a word which for the translator has only its shrunken dictionary meaning. The two Italian editions I used (see Bibliography) had such paraphrases for almost every obscure passage. On his way to a coffeehouse in the morning, the translator can have in his pocket the copy of a poem, footnoted with explications—almost as good as having a Michelangelo authority at his side. There, over his cappuccino, he can get a start on his translation, test his lines by mumbling them over on the walk home, then come back to his scribbles for as much of the day as he makes available, and perhaps for days thereafter. Michelangelo himself was a conscientious reviser; as many as a dozen versions of a poem, sometimes done over many years, have been found.

The translator is not likely to find his labor lighter than the poet found his own—nor any less pleasurable, as he reworks the furrows of his verse to richer loam.

The Long Beginning
1475–1532

N O OTHER ARTIST has had a life so fully documented as that of Michelangelo Buonarroti. Favored by and sometimes contending with a succession of seven popes in his almost ninety years, he left ample material for the several thousand books and articles his bibliographies now cata-logue. This present account is a foreshortened view of that life, its aim to provide the reader with a glimpse into the background of his poetry and the experience that engendered it.

The second of five brothers, Michelangelo was born in 1475 of a family previously distinguished but then in decline; it was to become one of his ambitions to restore the family for-tunes. His mother died when he was six; psychologists find significance in such early deprivation. On her death his care was entrusted to a wet nurse who was the daughter of a stonecutter; the poet Eugenio Montale thinks, perhaps fancifully, that fact fundamental in understanding not only his career as sculptor but also his lifelong struggle with the stringencies of verse. His father provided him with no formal education in literature; later in life an ignorance of Latin was to be an embarrassment to him among his learned friends.

Though against the will of his practical father, Michel-angelo made it plain that art was his early interest. Apprenticed at thirteen to the studio of the Ghirlandaio brothers, he left a year later to study among the sculptures Lorenzo de' Medici had collected in the Medici Gardens. There his youthful work so impressed the Magnificent One that Lorenzo took the boy into his own home, to be treated as a member of the family. There Michelangelo lived in fellowship with the most brilliant artists, poets, scholars and philosophers that Lorenzo, cele-brated as a poet himself, had been able to assemble. The con-trast between their worldly brilliance and the ominous thunder-ings of Savonarola, whose voice the young Michelangelo also heard and never forgot, would have deepened the division in his nature.

When he was only sixteen or seventeen, he did two reliefs so different from each other that they were prophetic of his entire career. One is the serene *Virgin of the Stairs,* of Christian

3

inspiration in the manner of Donatello; the other is the *Battle of the Centaurs,* of classic Roman inspiration, with its turmoil of brawny bodies struggling for their lives. Works so opposed, thinks de Tolnay (3), show Michelangelo's lifelong need "to express in disparate works the contrary tendencies of his being: the contemplative, seeking to evoke the internal image of beauty, and the active, seeking to incarnate the turbulent forces of his own temperament." De Tolnay (159) finds the same antagonism in his architecture, which he sees as "an incarnation of conflicting forces."

According to George Bull, Michelangelo's most recent biographer (1995), this ability "to embrace extremes in ideas and emotions" was a Florentine trait, which he sees also in Lorenzo, whose poems range from the salacious to the devout. A tension between extremes is felt also in Michelangelo's poetry, where often sentence takes issue with sentence, word confronts word, negations are negated. A similar embracing of extremes is shown by his ability to learn both from the classic agony of the *Laocoön,* unearthed in Rome in 1506, and from his grisly dissection of corpses awaiting burial in Florence.

We can guess that he began to write poetry while close to poets in the Palazzo Medici. Later, when about twenty-eight, his early biographer Condivi tells us, for a time he did almost nothing with chisel and brush, devoting his time instead to reading poetry and writing sonnets for his own pleasure. Likely enough he turned to verse because there were things he could not express through sculpture or frescoes: the *croce e delizia* of love, the remorse for a life he feared wasted, the thought of body and soul imperiled. In a letter of 1526, he told an associate that since the pen was bolder than the tongue, he was putting into written words what he dared not say.

The first poems we have of his seem to belong to his late twenties. When he wrote them, he was already a celebrity for statues admired then and now known everywhere: among them the tipsy *Bacchus,* the *Bruges Madonna,* the *Pietà* now behind bullet-proof glass in St. Peter's, and probably the *David* in Florence, delight of every tourist with a camera. He felt a kind of kinship with that heroic figure, a symbol of liberty, over twice

as tall as he was; on the back of sketches for it he wrote half a
dozen words that mean "David with his sling and I with my
bow," apparently a reference to the bow-like device that rotated
the sculptor's drill. He had commissions for other work, and
was soon to be summoned to Rome by the pope, who had fur-
ther grandeurs in mind for him. Few men have had such bril-
liant success when so young or more glorious prospects before
them. Yet the first poems (1 and 2) seem to come from the
depths of gloom, as if the poet were the sorriest of life's losers.
In 3, written when he was about thirty, he already sounds ad-
vanced in years. In 4 we have a poem which is totally at odds
with the circumstances of his life. In 1507 he was working in
Bologna on the colossal statue of Julius II. He disliked working
in bronze and had continual difficulties with the casting. "I'm
living as wretchedly as possible," he wrote his brother. "I work
day and night, and if I had this to do over I really think it would
be the death of me." Yet one month later, on the back of a letter
dated Christmas Eve, he wrote one of the most untroubled of
his poems (4), the description of a young beauty whose fash-
ionable apparel—as a sculptor would notice—revealed the con-
tours of her body, just as, some twenty-five years later, the stat-
ues of Lorenzo and Giuliano in the Medici Chapel would
dramatize the musculature beneath their regalia.

In an extended sonnet (5) we have the only poem in which
he describes doing a specific work of art. But how very different
the poem is from the circumstance that evoked it! In the verse
there is no hint of the beauty or grandeur of the Sistine epic—
nothing but a comic account of the artist's awkwardness and
irritation at having to paint a ceiling at all. In 6 he vents his
grievance at being snubbed, as he thought, by the pope; in 10
his indignation at the militarism, corruption, and greed that
plagued Rome at the time. Such outspokenness was rare in his
later poetry; he learned to be wary amid the violent crosscur-
rents of partisan strife in an age when a wrong decision could
threaten the life of even one as famous as he was.

From the other poems he wrote through the first third of
the century, one gets little idea of the drudgery, frustration, and
sometimes actual danger he had to contend with. His letters to

his father and his favorite brother express a continual solicitude about their welfare and the family finances, chiefly his responsibility. They also express frequent exasperation and outbursts of anger at their reactions and demands. Professionally, he was oppressed by overwork, caught between conflicting claims, often through his own fault, on his time and talent. His earliest surviving poem is written out on a sheet of architectural drawings for the projected tomb of Julius II, who had summoned him to Rome in 1505 with that in mind. This project, which his early biographer Condivi lamented as "the tragedy of the tomb," was a turbulent storm cloud lowering over him for the next four decades. Interrupting other commitments he had assumed but often neglected, it was designed and redesigned, begun, interrupted, modified, revived, and compromised as descendants of the della Rovere pope quarreled with the de' Medici popes, Leo X and Clement VII, and their families, who had rival claims on the talent of Michelangelo, for whom the burden of the tomb meant lingering guilt, possible financial obligations, and threats of legal action.

Beginning in 1518, his energies were given to planning a facade for San Lorenzo, the Medici church in Florence. Three years of hard work came to nothing when Pope Leo abruptly cancelled the project—little wonder the always touchy Michelangelo considered the blow to his pride a *vituperio grandissimo,* for which "gross insult" is a mild translation. Through most of the 1520s and beyond he worked on the dusky grandeur of the Medici Chapel and on the Laurentian Library, with its great cataract of a stairway. By 1525 about a hundred men were kept busy carrying out Michelangelo's plans for the library alone. There was far more to engage his energies than making plans on paper. He spent months on end in the mountains of Carrara and the rival quarries of Pietrasanta choosing and overseeing the quarrying of marble for his projects, building roads for the hazardous task of bringing it out, contracting haulers and shipowners, dealing with untrained workers and their labor problems. Toward the end of the tumultuous decade he was chosen governor-general in charge of improving the fortifications of

Florence against the expected siege by papal forces and their motley allies—risky work that strained his ties to both pope and his native city, involved death threats, a hairbreadth escape, charges of dereliction of duty. More than once his overburdened health protested. In 1528 his beloved brother died in his arms of the plague; his father died a few years later.

Little wonder that these thirty years produced few poems. More surprising is that there is no specific reference, after the early poems about papal Rome, to any of the ventures he was involved in. And what was he writing about in the leisure allowed him? About love, nearly always about love. Almost never about its *plaisir*; almost always about its *chagrin*. Even in the most assured of such poems (41) he sees himself "in the dungeon of love, by beauty bound." Perhaps written during the siege of Florence, the line reminds us of the *Slaves* he had done for the ill-fated tomb nearly twenty years before—struggling figures bound in the rock they never can writhe out of. Several poems caution about the grief love can entail:

> Flee from this Love, you lovers; flee the flame!
> The burning's bitter, and the trauma kills . . . (27)

One of the hazards, he felt, is that the lover can lose his identity in that of the person loved (8). Much later his friend Donato Giannotti described how Michelangelo excused himself from going to a congenial party because he was afraid of being attracted by someone there. "I am bound to fall in love with him, and I fall prey to him in such a manner that I am no longer my own: I am all his." Although in such Platonizing poems as 34 he sees human love and beauty as leading to the divine, he is also aware that tarrying on that upward path can lure one into sinfulness, especially (given the clerical and legal sanctions of that time) when his poetry would specify "him" and not "her" as love's object. "I live for sinning," he laments in 32, a conviction he develops in 51. But, as always, 25 shows he can take an opposite view:

> he who loves what nature gives commits no sin.

For Michelangelo, the risk and pain of love was as alluring as the joy in it:

> My death is what I live on; seems to me
> I thrive, and happily, on unhappiness,
> on death and anguish—if you live on less
> come join me in fire's mortal ecstasy. (56)

He was fifty-seven when he wrote those words, with only about fifty poems to show for the third of a century that covered the first period of his poetry—an average of less than two poems a year, half of them, like much of his sculpture, left unfinished.

1

A man who's happy many a year, one hour
—even less!—undoes; all's lost in grief and worry.
Another basks in his family name; that glory
is out in a flash as blacker heavens lour.

. . . .

. . . .

None so alive but death cuts short the story;
nothing so sweet but fortune turns it sour . . .

2

Brow burning, in cool gloom, as sundown shears
earth of its gala rays, alone I've lain.
Others lie here in pleasure, I in pain,
shaken, face down on earth, with sobs and tears.

3

I was happy, with fate favoring, to abide,
even to frustrate, Love, your savagery,
just to regret it now—in spite of me
these tears give proof how formidable you are.
   If your pitiless arrows missed by far
the target of my heart, long years ago,
revenge is yours; your eyes, so dazzling, throw
far deadlier darts my way, none going wide.
   How many a hidden net, how many a snare
the dapper songbird, by some twist of fate,
is spared from, with a sadder death in store.
   Such, ladies, as you see, is the fate I share:
Love kills me in a crueller way, so late
he assails, having spared me the long years before.

4

How joyfully it shows, the garland there,
flowers intertwining with the lady's tresses,
blossom with blossom jostling, as each finesses
for a better spot to kiss that golden head.

    All the day long the dress is comforted,
skirt flowing free from where the bodice tightens;
her collar's flounce ("spun gold" they call it) brightens
as it brushes on cheek, throat, shoulder, everywhere.

    That ribbon of gold lamé upon her breast
thrills even more with delight, seems all aquiver
at what it touches beneath the inserted lace;

    and the belt, demurely knotted, is so blest
it seems to sigh, "I could hug like this forever!"
Then what would they do—these arms!—in such embrace?

5

    A goiter it seems I got from this backward craning
like the cats get there in Lombardy, or wherever
—bad water, they say, from lapping their fetid river.
My belly, tugged under my chin, 's all out of whack.

    Beard points like a finger at heaven. Near the back
of my neck, skull scrapes where a hunchback's hump
        would be.
I'm pigeon-breasted, a harpy! Face dribbled—see?—
like a Byzantine floor, mosaic. From all this straining

    my guts and my hambones tangle, pretty near.
Thank God I can swivel my butt about for ballast.
Feet are out of sight; they just scuffle round, erratic.

    Up front my hide's tight elastic; in the rear
it's slack and droopy, except where crimps have callused.
I'm bent like a bow, half-round, type Asiatic.

    Not odd that what's on my mind,
when expressed, comes out weird, jumbled. Don't berate;
no gun with its barrel screwy can shoot straight.

Giovanni, come agitate
for my pride, my poor dead art! I don't belong!
Who's a painter? Me? No way! They've got me wrong.

6

If any of those old proverbs, lord, make sense
it's this: the one who's able, doesn't care to.
Such gossip, such crazy tales you've lent an ear to,
rewarding the one I know to be dead wrong.
I've been your loyal servant ever so long;
no sunbeam's more attentive to the sun.
Nothing to you, though, how my seasons run;
the more I drudge, the more I give offense.
My hope was, your eminence would help me rise,
that the scales of justice, the almighty sword
might still avail, not these same mouthy folk.
But virtue, its worth devalued in the skies,
is put out to grass on earth, where its reward
is scrounging for acorns from a mouldy oak.

7

Who's this that draws me forcibly to you?
Alas, alas, alas,
me, a free soul, so manacled, so bound?
If, without chains, you chain me as you do,
and, with no hands, no arms, tightly embrace,
then who's to save me from your lovely face?

8

O God, O God, O God, how can I be
no more my own? Not me?
Who stole my *me* away,
possessing it, to sway
all will of mine so I'm no longer me?

O God, O God, O God!
My skin unscathed, how may
this heart be wounded so?
What is it, Love, can dart
through eyes to the deep heart
to swell, as floods in tight arroyos grow,
this feverish overflow?

9

He Who made all there is, made every part
at first, then put those loveliest of all
together, to show what beauty's at His call,
as here, in this triumph of celestial art.

10

Chalices hammered into sword and helmet!
Christ's blood sold, slopped in palmfuls. With the yields
from commerce of cross and thorns, more lances, shields.
Still His long-suffering mercy falls like dew?
These lands are lands He'd better not come through.
If He did, His blood would boil, seething sky-high,
what with His flesh on sale, in good supply.
Virtue? Cast out. NO ENTRY signs repel it.
If losing money were the way I'm driven
—true, I've no work here—well, the triple hat
could freeze me out, no doubt, in Medusa's manner.
But now, if poverty's all the vogue in heaven,
how work the reversal of our grim estate,
as bloody flags take the wind out of heaven's banner?

11

How much less torment to breathe out my soul
this minute than time and again to die! Instead
of returning the love I feel, she'd have me dead.
What infinite sufferings weigh
upon my heart each moment I recall

one I so loved can love me not at all.
Why not then do away
with myself? She says, to aggravate my woe,
she loves not even herself—and maybe so.
Her chance of loving me then? The odds appall—
even to herself unloving! Harsh destiny:
likely enough, she'll be the death of me?

12

How could I, since it's so,
dare to endure, my love, with you away,
if, when we part, I'm too oppressed to pray
for grace? Those sighs, tears, sobbings—well I know—
that with my wretched heart attend on you,
prove, noble lady, and prove amply too
how close torment and death impend today.
Should you forget, though, when I'm far from you,
how fond a slave I was in times before,
this grieving heart I give you, mine no more.

13

Fame keeps the epitaphs where they lie; she moves
neither to front nor rear, because they are dead, and their
activity at an end.

14

The Day and the Night speak, and what they say is:
With our rapid course we have brought to his death Duke
Giuliano; it is certainly right that he take such vengeance
on us as he has taken. That vengeance is: Now that we
have put him to death, so in death he has left us in
darkness, and by closing his eyes has closed our own,
which no longer cast a brightness over earth. What might
he not have made of us then, if still alive?

15

Seeing I'm yours, I rouse me from afar
to come near the heaven I owe my being to.
With your allure the bait, I'm drawn to you,
tugged, as with hook and line poor fishes are.
And, as a heart torn two ways fails to show
much sign of life, to you both halves are given,
which leaves me poor—that's saying: much the same.
Souls, offered a choice, pick out the worthiest, so
not loving you's not life; that's how I'm driven.
I'm wood. You're wood, but gloriously aflame.

16

From one all loveliness and all allure,
from one, a fountain of mercy, comes my grief . . .

17

Rancorous heart, cruel, pitiless, though showing
what looks like sweetness—but the bitter core!
Your faith! as changeable as time, no more
likely to last than any springtime flower.
    Time moves and doles itself out, hour by hour;
no deadlier poison in our lives! Or say
it's like the sickle and we're like the hay

    .   .   .   .

    Faith is soon over. And no beauty lasts,
but, rapidly as faith does, wears away,
just as your sin would have my troubles fly

        .   .   .   .

    .   .   .   .

do with us always as the years go by.

Though shouldered from the road I chose
    when young,
I'd backtrack now. The byways I've explored!
All vain, in the trials and struggles I'm among.
The sea, the mountain, and the fiery sword!
Hemmed in by such as these, somehow I live.
But the one absconding with my wits won't give
me leave to have a go at the mountain road . . .

19

Fine lass or lady, they
by nature made, bar none,
were practice only, till she made the one
racking my heart with fire and ice today.
No man—it hurts to say—
was desolate as I:
throes, tears, sobs, soulful sigh.
For great effect, great cause. In grief's despite
I'm raised to heaven's height:
none ever felt, will feel, today's delight.

20

Sweeter your face than grapes are, stewed to mush;
looks like a snail had slicked it, to and fro,
the way it shines. Like radishes a-blush,
your cheeks. Teeth, sweet corn buttered, row with row.
On you the pope could get a heavy crush.
Your eyes! They're brown horse liniment aglow.
Hair pale as frizzy onions in their bin.
O love me, love! Or else you do me in.

In beauty you're more beauteously a beaut
than gilt St. Whozis in the sac·riss·tee.
Your mouth's a gunnysack of beans—but shoot!
so's mine. Ain't we some couple, you and me!
Your eyebrows, smudgy black as griddle soot,
twist like the huntin' bow of some Chinee.
At grub, your jowls, flour·spattered as your nose is,
are white and red, like grated cheese on roses.

When I peek down, eye hefting each bazoom,
I dream a dream of bulgy punkins sacked.
Like punk they light my fuse—hiss, szzz, ka·BOOM!
pooped as I am barn·cleaning. That's a fact.
If I still had, as once, my manly bloom,
for you I'd snub the loveliest—on your track
puff like a drooling pooch. Could marble match you,
you can bet your boots I'd whomp out one helluva statue!

21

Once born, death's our destination.
As the sun sends time a·flying
none survive in all creation.
End of laughter, end of sighing,
wit and witty comment vying,
famous family crests allying,
—shade in sunlight! wind·torn vapors!
We were fellow mortals: capers
like your own, carousing, weeping,
dusty relics of cremation.
All the one same destination.
We had eyes once, clear and merry,
deepset in the skull, a·glowing,
hollow grots now, black and scary
—such the rubble time comes towing.

What's to become of me? What's this you're doing
to my charred old heart you've made such ashes of?
Suppose you tell me, Love,
so I'll know how it stands with me, what trouble's brewing.

Surely my years have reached their destined end
like the arrow that, in its target, finds repose.
Fires that burned high should lie quiescent now.
I forgive you that storm of injuries you'd send;
they taught me to blunt the arrows, break the bows.
No room in my life for you now, though somehow
you fancy you'll find fresh ways to make me bow,
supposing my heart, so dazzled by your stunts,
wants what it wanted once?
The fact I can put you down so goes to show
I'm far from the man I was long years ago.

Perhaps you're hoping some new beauty's spell
will lure me back into the perilous trap
where even the hardiest have least will to fight.
No ordeal lasts when age begins to tell.
That's why I seem like ice the flames enwrap:
it shrinks, writhes to escape, but won't ignite.
I'm old. My sole defense is death, whose might
can ward off your brutal arm, your barbs that rain
their piercing pain on pain
—indulging none, indifferent to the great
in rank, in time, in stature, in estate.

Often my soul's in conference with death,
my fate the subject earnestly discussed.
New apprehensions threaten, every day,
as the body hankers for its dying breath,
and, by a mix of hope and dread nonplussed,
along the imagined road takes up its way.

Then, Love, you leap from the covert where you lay,
cocky, in armor, able-bodied, brave,
till all thoughts of the grave,
though urgent now, you rout—to promise me
green leaves and blossoms from a withered tree.
   What more can I do? Or should do? Having spent
all of my years retained in your domain,
have I a moment I can call my own?
What trickery, threat, or wily argument,
my thankless lord, could make me yours again?
O tongue of honey! your heart a graveyard stone!
Though recovered, I'd be shown
as shiftless, stupid, trustworthy no more,
since crawling back to what murdered me before.
   Earth has claws out for every creature born,
and mortal beauty must dwindle day by day.
The lover knows; he struggles—just the same
fails. Sin and vengeance are blood-brothers sworn.
The self-forgetful's the first to fling away
his soul and all in love's devastating flame.
And so, Love, you'd betray
me this last of days, which should be best? Your aim
is to plunge me, head over heels, into loss and shame?

23

   I was, for years and years now, wounded, killed
thousands of times, not counting blows, exhaustion,
by you, Love—all my fault, though. Hence the question:
grey-haired, I'm putty still as you'd seduce me?
   How many times you'd lasso me and loose me!
These poor old limbs—flanks furrowed by your spurring
till I'm not myself, or hardly, hot tears blurring
my eyes, down over throat and collar spilled.
   Too bad about you, Love! There's my last word,
deaf to your wheedling. The cruel bow you carry,

those arrows shot at random go to prove
    nothing. Termite or ripsaw'd be absurd
going after ashes. Absurd too, to harry
one who, lacking strength to carry on, can't move.

24

    I made my eyes an entryway for poison
when they let through your haughty hail of arrows;
for your sweet glance I hollowed nests and burrows
there in my memory's mine, secure forever.
    My breast I made a bellows to deliver
the sighs your flame had fueled, my heart the anvil . . .

25

    When with a clanking chain a master locks
in jail a slave with no amnesty, no hope,
the victim slumps and submits to it, will cope
with oppression rather than fussing to go free.
    So tiger and snake suffer captivity,
and the lion, rampageous, in rank jungles born.
So too the young artist, harried, worry-worn,
learns to endure from bearing with hard knocks.
    Only the fire of passion shuns compliance:
though it may leave green sapwood sere and dry,
in an old man's cooling heart it stays aglow;
    alluring him back to young love's wild defiance,
it renews, ignites, enraptures, kindles high
both heart and soul with the breath of love. And so
    don't you dare make a mot,
how in age the love of a lovely thing's beneath
what's decent—I'll say you're lying in your teeth!
    I'm not talking dreamy myth:
when a love's been weighed, assayed, reined nobly in,
he who loves what nature gives commits no sin.

Uproot a plant—there's no way it can seal
succulence in, once hoisted from its hutch;
what's it to do if warmth stirs, the least touch,
but parch and char and crackle into fire?
    So with my heart. Once stolen, my desire
is: Keeper, keep it, though in tears and flame.
Out of the proper home from which it came
is any injury not enough to kill?

27

Flee from this Love, you lovers; flee the flame!
The burning's bitter, and the trauma kills.
After the first encounter, ills on ills
there's no evading by vigor, wit, or distance.
    So flee! proof's everywhere of vain resistance
against his sharpened arrow, his mighty arm;
just look at me: what enormity of harm
awaits in Love's grim godforsaken game.
    Flee, and don't lose a moment. Now! No turning!
I thought I'd have my way with Love at will;
you see me chained to the stake, and burning, burning . . .

28

Because there's never a time I'm not enchanted
with your eyes—the memory of them, the expectation!—
which give me life, and make that life a pleasure,
it seems my fate and the way I am intended,
and nature too, O Love, and the mind's conviction,
my gaze to be fixed on you as life's one treasure.
And if I changed the way
that lets me live, then lay me underground.
No mercy's to be found
except what your eyes bestow.

Lord! but they're lovely though!
Not live for them's to be a babe unborn.
Born too late to see you
(I say between us two)
means: at the time he's born, right then he dies.
Not loving your fine eyes
is not to live at all . . .

29

All rage, all misery, all show of strength,
one armed with love can conquer, fortune too . . .

30

From eyes of my beloved one, come burning
flashes of fire so brilliant that through mine,
even closed tight, they stream, piercing the heart.
Off balance, poor Love's hurt:
bringing from you rays sheer and crystalline,
under my gloom he's burdened when returning.

31

Love in your eyes? No; life and death are there
(no other eyes so fair!)
as my own eyes discover. But the less
they seem to rage against me and oppress,
the fiercer burns their fire.
Besides, the love's more dire
whenever it seems friendlier than before.
When I would weigh, explore
what's bad, the good seems better momently.
Strange griefs tormenting me
still leave me panic-free.
If toil and penury
are a comfort here on earth where all's a curse,
then woe's my goal. Grow, woe! Grow worse and worse!

32

I live for sinning, for the self that dies,
my life being mine no more, this life in sin.
Heaven made me good; I dug the pit I'm in.
My will—of my own will—I've willed away,
    enslaved my liberty, made this case of clay
my very god—o miserable me!
And so I'm born for this! This ignominy! . . .

33

Were it true that, besides my own, another's arms
seemed to defend my every precious thing,
another's sword and lance, another's shield,
unless myself I'd grasp it, comes to nothing.
So very bad my way of life, it's taken
away the grace heaven pours on every place.

Like some old serpent through a straitened place,
I hope to pass, sloughing my shabby arms,
and hope my soul, restored to life, be taken
from habits long engrained, each mortal thing,
with cover now from a more trusty shield,
for, next to death, the whole world's less than nothing.

Love, I already feel I've sunk to nothing:
within me sin's entrenched in every place.
Strip me of me myself, and with your shield,
your rock, your genuine and gentle arms,
protect me from myself; each other thing's
as if it hadn't been, once quickly taken.

While soul from out of body's not yet taken,
Lord, Who could turn the universe to nothing,
creator, governor, king of each last thing,
how easily you'd find in me a place.

   · · · · · · · · · · · ·

   · · · · · · · · · · · ·

which are of each true man the truest arms
without which every man becomes as nothing . . .

34

Where my love lives is nowhere in my heart,
since, for the way I love you, heart's no home.
Such love as mine's not made of boorish loam
akin to sin and many a mouldy thought.

When our souls left the hand of God, love wrought
me with pure eye, you radiating light;
my yearning can't but see Him there, so bright
in—to our grief—your each poor mortal part.

Separate heat from fire—then you can prise
eternal beauty from my way of seeing,
which glorifies what resembles Him, here, now.

Since I behold all heaven in your eyes,
to get back there, where first we loved, I'm fleeing,
fevered with love, to the hospice of your brow.

35

The eyelid, shadowing, doesn't interfere
with vision; no difficulty for the eye
in gliding from side to side, the way being clear.

As slowly it stirs beneath the lid, we spy
merely a segment of its globe, and so
the serenity of its scope is lost thereby.

Covered, it doesn't dart much high or low;
less lid's apparent when the eye's agape;
unfurling, it leaves few crinkles there to show.

White's very white, black's black as a funeral drape
(if that can be) and lion-like the hue
of its fiber-to-fiber reticulated crepe.

Touching top and bottom fringes, if you do,
no way to distinguish yellow, black, or white . . .

My lover stole my heart, just over there
—so gently!—and stole much more, my life as well.
And there, all promise, first his fine eyes fell
on me, and there his turnabout meant *no*.

He manacled me there; there let me go;
there I bemoaned my luck; with anguished *eye*
watched, from this very rock, his last good-bye
as he took myself from me, bound who knows where.

37

In me there's only death; my life's in you;
time's marked and doled and measured at your will;
my life is longer, shorter at your nod;

your courtesy regales me through and through.
Blessed indeed the soul where time stands still:
prepared, through you, for contemplating God.

38

He who beguiles both time and death together
brings, through our eyes, what pleasure to the heart!
It's he who consoles me when the troubles start,
stays with me in affliction, hand in glove.

A wise and vital force, that one is Love
lifting my spirits—Love, my only care.
He tells me, "Good as dead, whoever there
boasts he's impregnable to my lofty pleasure."

What's Love? begotten first of beauty, blend
of imagination and vision in the heart,
to nobility and virtue bosom friend . . .

39

For a wound from the searing arrows Love lets fly
one cure: that they lodge the deeper in my heart.
None but my lord, though, has that archer's art
to make life exquisite through his exquisite pain.

Though mortal that first blow, to make all plain
Love, ever kind, sent with it his own squire
who said, "Be in love! Be on fire with love! That fire
feathers the flight to heaven when you die.

Love is the one that turned, from childhood on,
your eyes toward all the beauty they'd endure,
beauty that takes you straight from earth to heaven . . ."

40

When blithely Love would lift me up to heaven
with that lady's eyes—not eyes, no, with that sun—
half smiling, he rids my heart of every one
of its darker thoughts, enshrining there her face.

If I continued in such state of grace
my soul, that's all complaint when we're alone,
having with it, in the usual place it's known . . .

41

O noble soul, in whom, as mirrored, show
how in those limbs I love, lustrous and pure,
joint heaven and earth illustrate such allure
as not even their best can better, anywhere.

We hope and trust, lovable soul, that there
within you—your looks confirm it—have to be
love, goodness, mercy, of a rarity
never else seen with glamor blended so.

In the dungeon of love, by beauty bound, I lie;
my only hope, my assurance too, is there
in your glance, affectionate, rueful, true.

What custom, what power on earth would dare deny,
what callousness, now or ever, that death should spare
a creation as rare and beautiful as you?

Pray tell me, Love, if what my eyes can see
—that longed-for loveliness!—is really there,
or is mind fantasizing everywhere,
vivid as marble carved, her very face?

This you should know, who at her side keep pace,
much to my discomposure—and vexation.
Had I none to sigh for, though, worse deprivation.
Love like a low fire banked is not for me.

"The beauty in your wondering eye indeed
is hers alone, more glorious, if it take
love's way—eye, heart, to soul—once in whose skies

it's pure, divine, from earthly tincture freed.
Immortal things change others to their like,
and that's what enchanted first your mortal eyes."

43

My reason, out of sorts with me, deplores,
while I hold fast that love means happiness;
harshly, it documents love's storm and stress,
tells me to be myself: "No sense of shame?

Love's like the sun. Toy with that living flame
and it's your death. Not phoenix-fashion either."
But talk's no good. No help for one who'd rather
wallow in slime. Hands offered he ignores.

I know the harm I do me, see its truth.
But another heart within me rants, demanding
its own sweet will. I'm dead if I comply.

Dead also if I don't. It's death or death;
one I begrudge, one's past my understanding.
Caught in between, both soul and body die.

44

When to that beauty that I saw before
this life, I'd redirect my soul, my eyes
so glamorize *their* vision, the soul belies
its own, and shrinks back timorous, as abashed.

  Love, with the armory of tools it stashed
comes running back, so I won't break the ties . . .

45

It well may be, so vehement my sighing,
all fountains and all rivers had run dry,
but that their loss my tears kept resupplying.

  So with our eternal lanterns in the sky
—the hot, the cold—one gives what one has taken,
saving our world from extremity thereby.

  Thus in the lover's heart fierce flames are shaken
dangerously high by gusts of passion, till
quenched by the tears from sad eyes love-forsaken.

  Suffering and death, my heart's desire, can still
promise good days to come, long life ahead:
surely what gives such pleasure does no ill.

  Hence my soul's little dory hasn't sped,
as I'd prefer, to see you on that shore,
but leaves my body here a while instead.

  A grief too great keeps longer life in store,
as one the swifter runners leave behind
sees them, when sunset comes, arrive before.

  So kind a cruelty, courtesy unkind
have let me live but hustled you away,
unraveling, not undoing, the ties that bind,

  making off not just with memory, but, I'd say . . .

If my rough hammer shapes the obdurate stone
to a human figure, this or that one, say,
it's the wielder's fist, vision, and mind at play
that gives it momentum—another's, not its own.

But the heavenly hammer working by God's throne
by itself makes others and self as well. We know
it takes a hammer to make a hammer. So
the rest derive from that primal tool alone.

Since any stroke is mightier the higher
it's launched from over the forge, one kind and wise
has lately flown from mine to a loftier sphere.

My hammer is botched, unfinished in the fire
until God's workshop help him supervise
the tool of my craft, that alone he trued, down here.

47

When the occasioner of my many a sigh
was taken from earth, from sight, from self as well,
nature, who'd chosen earth as where he'd dwell,
was ashamed of the theft; and all who'd known him wept.

Our sun of suns! but now let no loose-lipped
bragging, like that for others gone, today
be heard from blustering death. Love won the day!
Love keeps him alive on earth, sainted on high.

This way—so death believed, conniving creature!—
would end the worldwide fanfare virtue sounded,
and so fob off his soul with a foul voucher.

Contrary, though, the effect: his file abounded
with brighter life than his life down here in nature.
Dead, he has heaven, who before was grounded.

48

Just as a flame, by wind and weather flailed,
flares up, so every virtue prized by heaven
is more resplendent, being more assailed . . .

49

Your beauty, Love, stuns mortal reckonings.
There's not a face among us can compare
with its image in the heart. You've kindled there
far different fire, fanned it with different wings.

50

What's to become of her, long years from now,
O Love, since time makes lank the fairest face?
Maybe her fame? That too fades—not a trace!—
faster by far than ever I'd allow.
    More and less . . .

51

Alas! Alas! for the way I've been betrayed
by rushing time! By a mirror too, that told,
had I conned it close, a story all too true.
It happens so, when regard's long overdue,
like mine, for life's last end. But time's parade
goes swiftly by, and overnight we're old.
Too late to repent, to set things right, to hold
counsel within, with death obtruding so.
My own self was my foe.
Of no avail how much I weep and sigh:
nothing annuls the waste of days gone by.
    Alas! Alas! reviewing all those days
there's not a one—not one!—I come on there,
in all that time, I truly call my own.
All bogus hope and vain desire! I've known

that my weeping, loving, burning, sighing ways
(no human passion then I didn't share!)
hog-tied me—don't I know!—remote from where
God's very truth must lie.
Deadly, the death I die!
What little time I had grows less and less.
Had I more, I'd be my old self, I confess.

    Worldweary, I plod on, no notion where,
but afraid because I *may* know. Time gone by
is a clue I cannot close my eyes to. So
as the time unpeels, sloughs off my pelt, I know
death and my soul match strength, contrary pair,
to see which determines where my fortunes lie.
If my mind's not gone awry
(and I pray the Lord I'm wrong)
I see me plunged headlong
in eternal pain for truth abused, when free
to choose. Any hope at all then, Lord, for me?

52

    Were one allowed to kill himself right here
in this world, thinking to return to heaven,
surely it's right that privilege be given
to a poor downtrodden dumb devoted creature.

    But since, unlike the phoenix, human nature
can't count on fiery solar resurrection,
hand lax and leaden leg, I take no action . . .

53

    Who rides by night on horseback, come the day
needs sleeptime, rest—or effort takes its toll.
And so I hope my own lord sees the way
    after such trials, to restore me, body and soul.
Only in good can evil make a stay;
often there's interchange though, role for role.

I do believe, if you were made of stone,
my love would prove so vehement, so true,
you'd soon come running to me on your own;
if you were dead, I'd charm replies from you;
if you were up in heaven, I'd sigh and moan
to win you back to earth—prayers helping too.
But you're alive! You're flesh and blood! You're here!
What can't a lover dream of, now you're near?

No option but traipse after where you go.
Commendable enterprise; I've no regret.
You're not some tailor's dummy, to and fro
dragged by just any whim. And don't forget
your soul's your own. Just keep it sound, for so
one day you'll choose to make me happier yet.
Two maxims: sampling sour, the lips close tight;
vipers, when handled gently, rarely bite.

No force prevails against a humble heart;
no cruelty resists the force of love;
no love but parries the most savage dart;
no grief but gladness gets the better of.
Great beauty, such as yours, gives earth a start!
Your heart's made like that beauty: from heaven above
both come. Straight scabbards, masterfully made,
never give housing to a crooked blade.

No way the long devotion I've been showing
won't capture your affection, just a bit.
Rare even among friends, and well worth knowing,
the kind of faith I give you. Count on it.

. . . .
. . . .
. . . .
. . . .

When there's a day it's clear we're not to meet,
well! I'm on pins and needles everywhere.
Then if I see you it's as great a treat
as, after days of fasting, tasty fare.

. . . .

. . . .

like one whose innards feel a desperate yen,
and goes—the worse before, the better then.

There's not a blessed day slips by without
my seeing her, or fancying she's nearby;
no oven, forge, or grill is so red-hot
it won't turn fiercer crimson if I sigh.
And when she happens near me, on the spot
sparks—look, it's like a foundry!—start to fly.
Having her near, I sputter chock-a-block;
Just me, I'd talk more sense, less poppycock.

She throws me, say, a smile, or I've a notion
she nods to me in passing on the street;
my fuse begins to smoulder—BOOM!—explosion!
I tell you, no bombarding could compete.
She asks the time of day; I'm all emotion;
voice quavers, wavers; I can hardly bleat.
Swollen desire collapses like a tent;
and hope goes hopeless, its last penny spent.

I throb with love I can't describe at all.
It lofts me skyward! Zodiacs I'm in!
When tongue, for glee, would raptly caterwaul,
it can't; no hole so vocal through my skin
the sound's more than mosquito-size. I crawl
away in shame, joy's resonance gone thin.
The power of love! Takes grace to show it right,
less clearly, though, the loftier its flight.

I think about the drift of days before
falling in love with you. Lone sands of time!
Then no one gave a glance at me. I'd snore
till noon, stare into space, daydream how I'm
to jostle past my fellow men, outsoar
the crowd. Or maybe vocalize in rhyme?
At least now I've a name, for good or ill.
They know me here. And here's the niche I fill.

Grape clusters, immature ones, when compelled
through bottle-necks, grow plump inside. Damp eyes
admit your image to my heart; it swelled
as grapes in glass do. Where your image lies
it pads me out, as fat makes sleeker pelt
(peel's pressured out by pushy pulp likewise).
So strait the eyes' damp inlet to the heart
no way—I don't dare think it—you'd depart.

How we inflate a ball is, blow in air.
A current the valve is ready to obey
lets in the breath; once in, it holds it there.
Exactly so these eyes of mine convey,
for keeps, your image to the soul. Compare
how ball and soul relate: game under way,
fists bong the ball, first bounce. Wow! See it fly!
Struck by your eyes, I'm booted up skyhigh.

A glamorous beauty thinks it not enough
to be praised by just one lover, seeing he
might die and—inconsiderate fellow!—snuff
her luster out. I dote deliriously,
but can't find words to tell of it. It's tough
for gimpy us to cavort in ecstasy.
Sun, now, won't stint its gift to one alone;
to each live eye on earth the glory's shown.

You make my heart—but how?—a raging pyre,
gliding through eyes, alas, forever wet.
They'd damp your glow, even sure-enough real fire.
And my defense? A paper parapet.
Fire ignite water? Then all things conspire
to keep me from the doom I'd die for yet.
So it's fight fire with fire. Strange: how explain
fire's the one analgesic for its pain?

55

Though quite expensive, look, I've bought you this:
a little *je ne sais quoi*, sweet-smelling too.
Now I can sniff my way, and never miss
your door, wherever I am, wherever you
happen to be. No longer compassless!
Hide if you want—all right. Play peekaboo,
I'll find you. Just carry this wherever you're at
and I'd nose you out in a whiff, though blind as a bat.

56

My death is what I live on; seems to me
I thrive, and happily, on unhappiness,
on death and anguish—if you live on less
come join me in fire's mortal ecstasy.

57

If I'm more alive because love burns and chars me,
as a fire, given wood or wind, feels new elation,
it's that he who lays me low is my salvation,
and invigorates the more, the more he scars me.

II

Three Loves

1532–1547

MICHELANGELO'S LITERARY OUTPUT almost quadrupled beginning in the fall of 1532, when, in his late fifties, he met the young Roman aristocrat Tommaso de' Cavalieri, then about twenty-three. The scholar Benedetto Varchi, in his talks about Michelangelo to the Florentine Academy in 1547, said that Cavalieri, "besides his incomparable physical beauty, had such charming ways, a mind so brilliant, and manners so winning that the better one knew him the more one loved him." Though he remained a loyal admirer and friend until he sat at the old man's deathbed, one has the impression that Cavalieri, later a family man and the father of the Florentine composer Emilio de' Cavalieri, was not homosexual, and, though flattered by the attention of one so great, was somewhat taken aback by the fervor of Michelangelo's approach. As early as the next New Year's Day, Michelangelo was offering to send him drawings; by July he wrote that "I could as soon forget your name as forget the food I live on—no, I could sooner forget the food, which, alas, nourishes only the body, than forget your name, which nourishes body and soul, filling each with such delight that I no longer feel sorrow nor am afraid of death, as long as I have you in my thoughts." The drawings he sent are probably his greatest. Done within a few months of his meeting Cavalieri, they are clues to the confusing tumult of his passion. All are based on Ovid: one on the story of Phaeton, struck by a bolt of lightning when he presumed to drive the chariot of the sun; another on that of Tityus, who for his attempted rape of a goddess was chained to a rock, his liver (the seat of lust) continually devoured by a vulture as it continually regenerated; and a third on that of Ganymede, the handsome boy carried off by an eagle to serve Zeus as cupbearer. Michelangelo may have paid Tommaso further homage by portraying him in the handsome face of Duke Giuliano, whose statue he was then working on for the Medici Chapel. In his poems, Michelangelo did not have recourse to mythology; the only myth recalled there is that of the phoenix, the fabulous bird restored to life in the very fire that destroyed it. Such fire is a recurring symbol in his love poems; in 97 he confesses that he is so inflammable in the presence of beauty that fire is his fate:

> With heart of sulphur, flesh of tinder too,
> bones like kindling, over these a soul
> with no direction, none, and no control,
> panting toward each impulse, each loveliness . . .
> then the fault's His who foredoomed it: fire's my fate.

The first sonnets that Michelangelo wrote for Cavalieri show he was conscious of his friend's reserve and aware also of the everpresent threat of gossip and scandal, if not actual danger from strictures of church and state. In the half-dozen sonnets of 1532 he is at pains to stress the innocence of his affection, especially against the "false tongues" and their slander (58). He is also uneasy because, innocent as he felt his passion to be, he feared the risk of serious sin, which he refers to in the prayerful lines of a sonnet probably of that year:

> O hoist me up from this doomed and evil slough
> of error: so close to death, from God so far. (66)

Over the next two years, some twenty of his best sonnets were inspired by his love for Cavalieri. Although, conflicted as always, he finds the experience of his love "bittersweet" and originating in a "yes-and-no emotion" (76), in his poetry he can still wish to have his "long desired sweet lord" in his "unworthy but eager arms, forever" (72). He is distressingly aware that age has made him less attractive and less capable of youthful ardor; he is tormented by the thought that his friend may abandon him, for "heaven's only where you are; else, total dark" (81).

Although many of the love poems of those years remain in the world of "handsome breast" and "eager arms," Michelangelo was also influenced by the Christian Neoplatonism of such thinkers as Marsilio Ficino, who, about a generation before, had written to a friend that "since nothing anywhere pleases except by its reflection of God, then it is God Himself Who pleases us in things that please." Ficino had been a resident in the Medici household; there the young Michelangelo might have heard him

talk about the *Symposium* of Plato, which he had translated, and
where there is a description of just such a love for "the divine
beauty, pure and clear and unalloyed, not clogged with the pol-
lutions of mortality and all the colors and vanities of human
life." It is such a conviction, writes Michelangelo, that justifies
his devotion to such young men as Cavalieri:

> where
> in the main God shows His glory, it's radiated
> veiled in some mortal form it shimmers through.
> And it's such I love, for the beauty mirrored there.
> (106)

So he can say of an attractive face that "often it lofts my soul
to God" and that there is "no other hint of heaven" on earth
except such beauty as his young friend embodies. Such con-
flicting emotions in the poetry remind us of the *contrapposto* of
his statues, the tension, close to torsion, with which the shoul-
ders strain one way, while face or knees are turned another. In
a poem which the handwriting seems to date among the pas-
sionate poems to Cavalieri, "one most powerful, prophetic, tor-
mented religious sonnet," says George Bull (p. 258) "erupted
into the sequence of early 1530 like an active volcano." Ago-
nized, as the first line itself is, it begins,

> I wish I'd want what I don't want, Lord, at all . . . (87)

Yet somewhat later, even as his passion seemed to be cooling,
he could write the frankest avowal of his love in a sonnet that
ends, not without self-abasement, with a pun on the name of
Cavalieri—the only time it is mentioned in the poems:

> If being bested and bound is my delight,
> no wonder I'm made a prisoner, nude, alone,
> as a cavalier in armor turns the key. (98)

His pleasure in being "bested and bound" in love is nowhere
more eloquently expressed than in the statue Vasari was to call
Victory. Though its dating is uncertain, some would assign it to
1533–34, Michelangelo's last years in Florence. In the statue a
nobly muscled and elegantly aloof young man presses one bent

knee on the crouching back of a submissive older man, bearded like Michelangelo.

After the rich outpouring of love poetry through 1533 and 1534, the poems for Cavalieri become fewer. In 95 he asks to have back the tears, the sighs, the wasted footsteps, so that they can be directed toward another love, perhaps Febo di Poggio, the young man whom E. H. Ramsden, the editor of Michelangelo's letters, characterizes (somewhat naively) as "selfish and self-seeking . . . wholly unworthy of Michelangelo's fatherly interest and affection." His name (Apollo of the Hill) afforded the poet rich material for the kind of pun he favored (99 and 100). In other poems for Cavalieri, physical passion is now downplayed: soul alone should be the object of love:

> My love's aflame only for this, whose worth
> is beyond your classic beauty that takes the eye . . .
> (106)

In 109 "sensual bliss" is discredited for its "core of ash and gall," a new awareness that Michelangelo finds

> Like a biting lash, the awareness! And the pain!

Though during these years his most passionate poetry was inspired by his love, that was not his only inspiration. In years often feverish and troubled, he found time for the dozen or so stanzas of *ottava rima* on the nature of love, ranging from earnest emotion to bizarre foolery (54) and for the even longer sequence on the pleasures and purity of country life (67) and his satiric fantasy about the giants (68). The death of his father, probably in 1531, recalling that of his favorite brother a few years earlier, was lamented in the unfinished *terza rima* of 86. Different from these were the rowdy high spirits, in-jokes and literary allusions of the letter to the burlesque poet Berni (85). Different from all were his paradoxical meditations on night (101–4), his favorite of the four times of day whose statues lacked his finishing touches in the Medici Chapel. These and other works in Florence were abandoned when he moved to Rome in September 1534, partly out of dislike and fear of Duke

Alessandro de' Medici and his regime, partly to be near Ca-
valieri and the site of his grand new project: a Sistine fresco of
the *Last Judgment.*

It was in Rome in 1536, a few months after starting work
on the fresco, that he met Vittoria Colonna, the other great
love of his life. A daughter of the Grand Constable of the King-
dom of Naples and one of the most distinguished women of her
time, she had been much courted after the wartime death of
the dashing officer she had married at nineteen. But she never
remarried, loyal to the memory of a husband she recalled in
poems by turns amorous and spiritual. In an age of religious
upheaval (Luther had posted his theses on the church door in
1518) she was devoted to church reform and lived much of her
later life in convents. Many of her friends were to become Prot-
estants, though she did not. By die-hard conservatives she was
eyed with suspicion; Michelangelo's association with her em-
broiled him in their hostility.

Her poetry, her religious beliefs, and her distinction would
all have attracted Michelangelo. That year the pope himself had
given a reception in her honor; the emperor, when in Rome,
had paid her a visit. Almost immediately the poems inspired by
her began. She was not beautiful, as more than one of those
who knew her have ungallantly remarked. But, looking beyond
appearance, Michelangelo found her beautiful (in a somewhat
masculine way); he probably overrated her poetry; more and
more he came to share her radical belief that salvation could
come through faith alone (Luther's *fide sola*), thanks to Christ's
sacrifice of blood on the cross and not through any work of
man—a belief some think he dramatized over the next five years
in the *Last Judgment,* its stern Christ seeming to choose those
He would and to reject those who thought they could storm
heaven on their own. (But see note to 289). Though Vittoria
sounds rather like a mother superior, she must have been rich
in worldly wisdom and social charm. Raised among soldiers in
an aristocratic world of high-powered intrigue, she had become
briefly involved when her brother took arms against the pope
himself. According to Francisco de Holanda, the Portuguese
painter who was several times in the company of both Vittoria

and Michelangelo, she may even have had a playful sense of humor. Once, when de Holanda had spoken eloquently about painting, Vittoria slyly remarked that maybe she should divorce Michelangelo and go back to Portugal with the younger man. Though out of Rome for about half of the years she knew Michelangelo, she is reported to have made frequent trips to see him. Perhaps the first intelligent and sympathetic woman the motherless Michelangelo had the good luck to meet, she was a resource and a consolation to him during the years they knew each other.

During all of those years Michelangelo's painting was ardently religious. The *Last Judgment*, begun in the year of their meeting, was finished in 1541. Immediately he began work on the Pauline frescoes for the pope's private chapel: the first showing the conversion of a stunned St. Paul, the second, the crucifixion of St. Peter. That whole time he was hounded by the kind of worry and distraction he was never without: there were family financial problems in Florence; a contract he had made for the tomb of Julius II had expired with little or nothing done, and a new contract had to be contrived; much maneuvering led to the completion of the shrunken tomb in 1545. In 1537 his old enemy, Duke Alessandro, had been assassinated; the event occasioned debate about when it was justifiable to kill a tyrant. In 1539 a friend suggested he do a bust of Brutus, thought noble by some because he had killed the tyrant Caesar. Michelangelo had nearly finished the impressive work when he had second thoughts about the *Et tu, Brute!* Cosimo de' Medici's autocratic rule in once republican Florence distressed him. Though discreet in political matters, in 1545 or 1546 he wrote his famous quatrain for the statue of *Night* in the Medici Chapel: it is sweet, he has her say, to sleep, an insensate thing of stone, in times so evil (247). Probably in the same year he wrote the two sonnets in praise of Dante (248 and 250), both implying censure of his native city. In 1544 and again the next year he was seriously ill, taken in and cared for by his friend Luigi del Riccio, who had become a sort of business manager and literary adviser a few years before. In 1544 del Riccio's popular young nephew, Cecchino Bracci, had died; Michelangelo then wrote his fifty or so little poems in memory of the handsome child.

Most of his literary energy during these years went into the poems for Vittoria Colonna, to whom, Eugenio Montale believes, the most tender and passionate of his love poems were written. Others think that although these are some of his finest poems—loving poems, poems *about* love—they are not exactly "love poems," and that, as Glauco Cambon says (66), they seem to be to a woman who has "the cold androgynous beauty of some of his Madonnas."

The devout Vittoria was not to be addressed in the language he had used for the young man he had loved. There is no more "wild desire" or "eager arms" embracing (98 and 72), nothing of "the senses' rapturous burning" (93). These are poems in which it is "forbidden to bring hands, arms to rendezvous," and only our eyes, the purest agents of the spirit, can participate (166). In this, one of the most aspiring of the sonnets, the poet prays that his whole physical being, like some creation of Odilon Redon, may be turned into "all eye, to delight, the whole of me, in you."

In earlier love poems, Michelangelo had feared to lose his identity, his very self, in that of the person loved. Not so with his new love, whom he implores to "save me from that old me, self's black abyss" (235). He almost grovels, though blissfully, in his inferiority to her; not even his "talent and art" can match her own heavenly gifts to him (159). Time and again he begs her to make a better man of him, perhaps through communications like that of her poetry:

Here's the blank page I lay
before your sacred ink . . . (162)

One of his first poems to her asks that she redesign him to her liking, as on blank paper or stone he can write or carve what he would have there. Such reference to his art is sustained and developed in at least half a dozen of his later and best-known poems. In the ones for Cavalieri the only mention of art concerns his "dubious drawings" (79), the possibly salacious mythological subjects from Ovid, seen as confessional of his infatuation. The drawings he sends to her are centered on the passion of Christ.

His allusions to the craft he knows best bolster his devotion:

> I carved the statue, but she's heaven's own art . . .
>   (240)

Incorporating the solidity of sculpture gives body to poems that might otherwise seem too lost in celestial vapors:

> Where I lack, you add; where I'm rough, you file
>   and gloss
> in your kindly care for me . . . (236)

One of his best ones concludes with a reference to the power of art:

> Though we're dead a thousand years, still men
>   can see
> how beautiful you were; I, how much duller,
> and yet how far from a fool in loving you. (239)

Vittoria's death in 1547 stirred him to some of his most heartfelt and moving poems. It was probably not long afterward that he expressed his longing for their times together in terms he might not have dared direct to her living ear:

> Bring back the day the reins hung slack and free
> and love rode roughshod over me . . . (272)

The sonnet concludes with an image of life without her:

> A log burned through won't catch; I'm all dead embers.

Michelangelo saw in himself and in the world he knew an interplay of opposites. There is no stranger revelation of the duality within him than that during the very years he was writing his exalted sonnets to a lady whose beauty signaled him the way to heaven, he was writing just as many poems, madrigals more often than sonnets, to the one his historians call "the lady

beautiful and cruel." In every way she was Vittoria's opposite:
her fascinating physical beauty veiled something like indifference, if not contempt, for her poet; she offered nothing in the way of heavenly direction. In her company hell itself was an acceptable possibility (139 and 140). If by any chance she could be in heaven with him, her beauty would upstage that of God Himself (140). Though with her he felt old and ugly, he seemed to enjoy subjecting himself to her abuse, all the more since his misery brought a brighter glow to her lovely cheeks. The faintest chance that she might return his affection was enough; that illusion was more consoling than the brutal reality:

better nurse a delicious doubt than gag on truth. (141)

Even her falsity brought him happiness:

I still
revel even as you deceive me. Always will. (174)

The awareness of his ugliness next to her beauty gave him pleasure, since the uglier he looked the more beautiful it made her seem (172). What would Vittoria Colonna, prayerful before the drawings of the crucifixion that he sent her, have thought of all this? Michelangelo made no effort to conceal his poems of bedeviled love: when in the 1540s he and two friends were preparing his poems for publication, he chose for inclusion at least as many for "the lady beautiful and cruel" as for Vittoria Colonna. One has to admit that some of them are more lively, more readable, more down to an earth we know, than certain of the poems yearning heavenward.

And who was the glamorous lady? There are no clues in the poems themselves, no letters that testify to such an attachment, no mention of her by friends or early biographers. No evidence, in short, that she existed at all. Not that she was pure fantasy: she did embody something very real in the imagination of Michelangelo: all of the rebuffs and frustrations that the oversensitive poet, nearing seventy, felt he had suffered at the hands of those he loved. Perhaps, as some think, she was even a version of Vittoria herself, who, devoted to religion and spending much of her time in convents, could hardly have given herself, heart and soul, to a man she truly admired and cared for. Or perhaps Michelangelo, spiritually in love with Vittoria, represents in his beautiful and chilly phantom the other face of love—unattainable love at a distance, which, Montale reminds us, was the *amor de lonh* of the Provençal poets of centuries before. Or was she not the "she" of the poems at all, but a cover-up for some possibly emended "he" past and present? All we can be sure of is the poetry itself, impossible to date precisely, though all written from the years of his first poems to Vittoria until about the time of her death.

The fifteen years of this second period of his poetry, from his fifty-seventh to his seventy-second year, produced among its two hundred poems much of his most powerful work. Besides the love poems to a man, a woman, and a vexing phantom, he made time in his busy life for other literary duties and diversions: there are the fifty little quatrains for Cecchino Bracci (179–228); the two politically slanted sonnets about Dante (248 and 250); the allegorical lines on Florence (249). As his sculpture may have influenced the chiseled diction of his sonnets, so all of these poems in *ottava rima* and *terza rima* may have influenced his art. Of the *Last Judgment*, de Tolnay (54) has written that "a rhythm comparable to that of the verses of a poem organizes the whole."

58

If longings for the immortal, which exalt
and chasten the thoughts of others, could disclose
my own, then it could be, in the house Love knows,
they'd arouse a pity in the pitiless king.

But since the soul, by heaven's provisioning,
has long to live, while the brief body dies,
sense cannot fully praise, can't fitly prize
soul seen as a blur at best—our eye at fault.

The worse for me and for innocent desire
aflame in my heart! For now how make it clear
to those who project themselves in others? My grief

is for precious hours spent queasily with my sire,
too attentive, he, to the false tongues at his ear.
Not a lie of sorts, to reject a sound belief?

59

If pure devotion, passion without stain,
if one sole fortune rules an affectionate pair,
if the other's trouble each hastens to share,
if in two hearts one spirit and one will,

if in two bodies there's one soul, a-thrill
for eternity, wings plumed for heaven above,
if, with one thrust, one golden arrow, Love
drives deep in the breasts of both his raging pain;

if what they love's not self but only other,
so precious their glee and ecstasy they must
aspire to the one same final end, those two:

thousands of *ifs* (their love-knot such) together
can't equal love's hundredth part, so true their trust.
Even this, though, a lover's dudgeon could undo.

You know, my lord, that I too know you know
I like my being by you. You know why.
And you know I know too you know that I
am this same I I am. So: why not meet?
　　You give me hope as true, I trust, as sweet.
If the great desire I'm blessed with now is true,
let the wall come tumbling down between those two.
There's twice the mischief in stress hidden so.
　　If what I love in you, dearest of lords,
is what you love within yourself, why then
no umbrage. We've two souls here, both in love.
Your handsome face—what I learn from it, what rewards
I'd have of it, that's obscure to worldly men.
Beyond death, though, they'll learn. In heaven above.

61

If, when it caught my eye first, I'd been bolder,
trusting to find new life in the burning sun
of a phoenix so divine (for such was done
to the phoenix's self in age) whose fire I feel,
　　then, quick as roebuck, leopard, lynx can wheel
toward the mark of its lust or rage, or away from danger,
so I, to your laugh, your ways, your truth no stranger,
would have sped. As now I do, but slower . . . older . . .
　　What point, though, in still bemoaning, now I see
in the eyes of this blithe angel, nonpareil,
my rest, my quiet haven, my heaven's height?
　　To have seen, to have heard him earlier, worse for me,
since now, in our closer bond—so time would tell—
he's given me wings to track his soul's own flight.

62

Only with fire can men at forge and flue
work iron after the concept they design;
without such fire, no artisan can refine
gold to its true allure; fire makes it glorious.

Nor does the fabled phoenix show victorious
except in flame; so I, in fire to die,
hope for a bright survival in the sky
with those whom death exalts, time's gentle to.

Fortune's my friend. The fire I'm speaking of
is a glow deep inside to revitalize me
close as I am to death, long time expected.

Fire by its very nature's borne above
to its proper element; fire deifies me;
I'm fire, and so where but up to heaven directed?

63

So fond is fire of the frigid stone it waits
within that, struck by steel, it glories round it,
gives it new life, having calcined it and ground it
to a stuff that mortars stone jam-packed forever.

If fire can't conquer it, summer, winter never
can dislodge it, and its worth accrues the more,
as a soul, in purgatory cleansed, will soar
to share with the high and holy their estate.

There's a vein of flame deep in me. If desire
foments it to flare and kindle me, all the same,
though burnt, done for, I'll live, to love beholden.

For, charred to cinder and smoke, confirmed in fire,
still alive, I live forever: immortal flame
struck not by glancing steel, but a glance more golden.

64

If fire can melt down steel and shatter flint
—those two, so tough within, its own begetter—
will a fire far worse than hell's treat any better
its contrary; dried out straw, mere wispy lint?

65

Just when I'm lost in adoration of you
the memories of my misery return,
reminding me through tears: "Unless one burn
fiercely in love, it isn't love. I burn!"
    But I, though, make a shield from all that crew . . .

66

Maybe, so I'd look kindly on souls in need,
not gloat over folk less lucky when they tumbled,
my own soul, sure of itself, abruptly stumbled,
being quite above advice, smug, well-reputed.
    What soldier under an earthly flag recruited
who—forget winning! only thinks survive!—
could, from war's hostile clangor, slink alive,
unless Your preponderant mercy intercede?
    O flesh, O blood, O agony, crucial wood,
there's justification of my sin through You,
sin ours from birth, and my father's too. You are
    boundless in mercy and sole source of good;
O hoist me up from this doomed and evil slough
of error: so close to death, from God so far.

A new and more commendable delight,
to watch the goats as dizzily they climb,
browsing on this or that or the other height,
their shepherd meanwhile trolling, in rough rhyme,
his country lovesong down below—he might
loll by a stream, or stroll, flute keeping time.
He eyes his lady-love (O heart of stone!)
with pigs, beneath an oak tree, posed alone.

One pleasure more, to see, snug on a hill,
their modest little hut of thatch and sod,
lunch being readied where a makeshift grill
is lit beneath a favorite beech; with prod
a chuckling youngster slops the porkers; still
another schools the donkey for his load.
Old grandpa, snoozing, with few words to say,
basks in the dooryard sunshine through midday.

Now look inside the little house—what's there?
They don't have any money—what's it for?
By day they go out plowing; the home's bare;
you see all their possessions from the door.
They don't have locks; where what's to lose, why care?
All's open, as it was long years before.
Chores done, they munch on crispy acorns, then
content, sleep cozily on straw. Amen.

Nothing to envy, so no envy's here;
what's to be proud of but their honest pride?
Greed? to enjoy the woodland meadows near,
no matter whose, with pinks and daisies pied.
Their prize possession is their plow and gear;
its shining steel commends them. And inside
they've baskets—two—that do for chiffoniers.
Gold vessels, hardly! Hoes, spades, pruner's shears.

O greed with bleary eye! O witless wits!
that still abuse good nature's charity.
Grubbing for wealth, for grand estates, for bits
of dirty earth—fierce pride's your deity.
To loll and letch, your mentors. Envy fits
you with all means to be unneighborly.
You fail to note, your rabid fever such,
our days aren't many, and our needs not much.

Those men of long ago, of sounder sight,
ate acorns and drank water from the spring.
Make those your model, mirror, guide and light
against voluptuous play, fine palating.
Listen to what I'm saying now: in spite
of emperies worldwide, the greatest king
hankers for this or that: life's Chinese box.
The plowman's cozier with his trusty ox.

Adorned with gold and jewels, preoccupied,
see *Wealth* go creeping by with worried brow,
vexed by the wind and rain, by time and tide,
querying signs and portents with "How now?"
But jolly *Poverty* goes well supplied
with unsought treasure, slighting "When?" and "How?"
Snug in the woods, in rough and comfy duds,
no stress; not care's nor duty's nor bad blood's.

Debits, receipts, those dealings strange and weird,
what's better and what's worse, fine points of art
mean nothing to those farm-folk. Country-reared,
it's water, grass, and milk-cows stir their heart.
Their callused palms, their rural tunes appeared
to them as basic as, to some, the chart
clerks keep, or usurers (more every day!).
They follow as the flow goes, come what may.

The plowman loves, fears, honors God; he prays
too for his grain, his labor, goats and mule;
with faith, with hope, his trusting eyes he'll raise
in prayer for the calving cow, the burly bull.
Doubt, Maybe, How and *Why* can scarcely faze
or warp one never subject to their rule.
He'll beg the Lord and heaven their help to send;
one he'll bind to himself, the other bend.

Doubt we depict as well cuirassed but lame,
a grasshopper, you'd think, to see him leap;
he's in a twitter always, much the same
as, in a marsh, thin reeds the breezes sweep.
And *Why's* a skinny one, who always came
keys at his belt, but each bent out of shape.
None fit in any lock; he'll force them all.
He walks by night; murk follows at his call.

How and *Maybe* are cousins, both the two
so tall that, stretching, they can touch the sun;
a feat that both, it seems, delight to do,
so, naturally, it blinded either one.
Their bulky breasts won't let the sunlight through
to shine on cities—the bright day's undone.
They walk, through stony land, roads never straight,
test with their touch which rocks can bear their weight.

But *Truth* goes off poor, naked, all alone,
though held in high regard by simple folk;
one eye it has, pure, luminous; its own
body is gold, its heart a diamond. Stroke
after cruel stroke but doubles its renown;
killed in one place, in hundreds it awoke.
To look at, though its color's fresh and green,
it proves to friends what candor's meant to mean.

Eyes toward the earth, as if in modesty,
in cloth of gold, embroidered and bizarre,
goes *Falsehood;* to the just, sworn enemy.
Hypocrite! currying friendship near and far.
Its heart all ice, so sun it has to flee,
haunting the court, where darkest shadows are.
For helpers and best friends, has always by
Deception, Wrangling—and its love, the *Lie.*

There's *Flattery* too; no end of trouble, she!
a buxom minx and cunning as they come;
her silks all chatoyant, a sight to see—
no mead in May's so wildly frolicsome.
What *Flattery* wants, then *Flattery* gets; her plea
plays on your pleasure always—else she's dumb.
If no cajolery works, then tears coerce.
Her eyes adore, her fingers pick your purse.

To court's skullduggery she's mother. Yes,
and wet nurse too. There's malice in her milk,
her misbegotten seed she'll feed, caress . . .

68

Then there's this giant—tall! So tall he can't
see us—from where his eyes are—way down here.
Enormous feet, which many a time he'd plant
plumb on some town and scuff it to a smear.
High as the sun he'd like to gallivant
on towers he'd build, but never sees it clear.
Though great the strength his bulky limbs reveal,
one eye is all he has, and—in his heel!

That's why he only sees what's just behind.
Like a great prow in heaven moves his chin.
As for his legs, a two-day's march, we find,
might cover what we see of hairy skin.
Above, no seasonal change of any kind
he feels; fair weather's all he's ever in.
Up there, his forehead's level with the sky;
his big feet level mountains, shuffling by.

He feels sierras shift beneath his tread
the way we'd feel some tiny grains of sand.
The hairy jungles on his shanks have bred
rare monsters, never seen on sea or land.
Where we see whale he sees a fly instead.
He's only vexed when made to raise a hand
to wipe away a tear if gusty sky
blows smoke or dust or litter in his eye.

With him, a sluggish gross old swollen hag
who breast-feeds—yes!—this horrifying lout,
egging him on to rage, rampage, and brag,
mindless and blind, whatever he's about.
Alone, she keeps her grotto on a crag,
gaunt rocks around, walls threatening all, "Keep out!"
There when he'll doze, she, squatting on dark earth,
hatches grand plans for universal dearth.

She's pale—say yellowish-pale—her weighty womb
betokening something of her lord's ado.
Folk's woe is her delight, their glee her gloom;
day, night she hogs down victuals, never through.
No goal and no control, and that's her doom.
Hates others; doesn't love herself though—phew!
Oceans and mountains in her gut she's thrown;
her grip's of iron, but her heart of stone.

They've cast their seven offspring far and wide
to scour the whole of earth, from pole to pole;
only against the just their spite's applied.
Each ogre has a thousand heads; the toll
they take on earth makes hell's great portals slide
busily back and forth, soul after soul.
Slowly their snaky limbs around us clinch,
as ivy clamps on brickwork, inch by inch.

69

Nature knows what it's doing: one cruel as you
needs beauty in equal measure with disdain;
contraries should balance, neither more nor less.
    Your face with all its glamor—since they do—
can, with a touch of sweetness, soothe my pain:
a bit less the ache, a bit more love's blessedness.

70

O cruel star, or say instead, cruel will,
leaving impotent my own will, as if bound:
there's no bright star concerned for me in heaven
ever since the day my sail unfurled, swung free,
and forth, a wanderer and adrift, I went,
light ship tossed to and fro by all the winds.

    Worn out now, here I am; in torrid winds
I've had to launch my skiff, and, weak of will,
plow the same surges where I always went.
Down here we snatch the fruit which, mischief-bound,
we stole from the Tree high up, our options free,
and that way lost the inheritance of heaven.

Here I'm not steered or driven full-sail by heaven,
but by these rough and mighty offshore winds,
now backed by a force unknown, set somehow free
against me—who knows why?—to abduct my will.
In another's net, not mine alone, I'm bound.
My fault, perhaps, where unwittingly I went?

Cursed be the day that such a way I went
in blind obedience to a sign from heaven!
Not that I think a zodiac keeps me bound
and impels the soul, amid contrarious winds,
to forsake our generous heritage, free will.
It's trying times, we learn, that prove us free.

So then, if passionate heartache dared to free
sighs it suppressed, or if prayerfully I went
through chafing winds, to Whatever's beyond our will,
something in pity of those chafing winds
sees, hears, and feels. I sense a friendly heaven.
But same hands can't unbind the self they bound.

He's paralyzed himself, who chose being bound;
binding himself, himself he can't set free.
If, as a tree grows straight and true toward heaven,
it ever was toward you, my Lord, I went,
let me return, unbuffeted by winds,
to shield with Your grander purpose my weak will.

The one who freed and bound again my will,
him I was blown to by tumultuous winds
—he was your gift. Avenge me now, high heaven!

71

I have your letter, thank you, as received,
and have read it many times, at least a score.
It's clear you don't need sharper teeth, any more

than one stuffed to the gills needs food. And since
    I saw you last I'm assured, having more than hints,
you have Cain the killer himself for ancestor,
and that in your blood genetic traits still fester:
if fortune befalls another, you feel aggrieved.
    Jealous, conceited, enemies of heaven,
a neighbor's kindness sets your teeth on edge,
you Pistoians, self-destructive, eye askance
    on every virtue. The great Poet even
saw the truth. Fix that in your memory, and don't hedge.
If you praise my Florence, I know it's song-and-dance.
    Florence! our town enchants!
How precious a jewel you'll never comprehend.
That takes some brains. We can count you out there, friend.

72

    If, through our eyes, the heart's seen in the face,
more evidence who needs, clearly to show
the fire within? Let that do, my lord, that glow
as warrant to make bold to ask your favor.
    Perhaps your soul, loyal, less like to waver
than I imagine, assays my honest flame
and, pitying, finds it true—no cause for blame.
"Ask and it shall be given," in that case.
    O day of bliss, if such can be assured!
Let the clock-hands end their circling; in accord
sun cease his ancient roundabout endeavor,
    so I might have, certain-sure—though not procured
by my own worth—my long desired sweet lord,
in my unworthy but eager arms, forever.

73

    Now that I'm banned and routed from the fire
nothing to do but die, though safety's here.
I thrive on fiery food. Others come near
such fare and drop down dead. I'm all the spryer.

I weep, I burn—burn up!—my heart thereby
finds nourishment to live. O lucky me!
Who else can thrive on his mortality
as I do now on anguish and distress?
    Ah, love's cruel archer, deftly you assess
the times to quiet, with your athlete's hand,
our fleeting hours of torment. Understand:
who lives on death is meant never to die.

75

    Too much! the way he flaunts himself around,
knocking folks dead, he's such a handsome sight.
. . . .

showing off, gallivanting on the town.
    Too much! the way he makes the sun dim down
by batting his brighter eyes, till noon seems night.
And then his song, his laugh! The pure delight
dumbfounds. O he's a prince! Get out the crown!

76

    Whether or not the light I long for, sent
from its first maker, set my soul aglow,
or a memory, maybe, of those I used to know
—one, say, especially lovely—floods my heart;
    of someone just heard of once, a dream in part,
an apparition haunting both heart and eye,
a searing memory of who knows what, or why—
perhaps of the one for whom these tears are meant.
    What I feel, what I want, who'll show the way,
is beyond me. Where to look I've not a notion
myself—not if someone pointed where it lies.
    It began, my lord—and so bittersweet—the day
I saw you, and rocked with a yes-and-no emotion.
No question about the cause of it. Your eyes.

Supposing the passionate fire your eyes enkindle
were omnipotent as the beauty there aglow,
no land on earth, deep under ice and snow,
wouldn't spray out flame, as burning arrows do.

But heaven, compassionate with our troubles, to
the glamor it lavished—yours!—makes us half-blind,
giving instead, with our harsh life in mind,
more tranquil glimmers such as flesh can handle.
Compared to your beauty's blaze, my heart seems cold?
Only as much heaven as can fill the eye
sets the weak soul afire, poor lovers yearning.

That happens, my lord, in our regard: I'm old.
If I don't take instant fire, seem like to die,
it's because just scattered scraps are left for burning.

78

From grief I cherished to a rueful laugh,
from peace eternal to a truce with time
I've tumbled. Where the truth keeps mum, then I'm
spellbound by what takes over, the five senses.

My heart's to blame? Or your face for what dispenses
pain that turns all the sweeter with its growth?
Or is love's torch at fault, glowing in both
those eyes that you stole from heaven, like enough?

Your beauty was never born of this world's weather.
It's heavenly born, from heaven to earth imported.
Though much I've lost, I glory and burn anew;

being close to you, I'm me, and can't be other.
These deadly weapons against me heaven assorted;
then if I die, who did it—you? Or You?

Blissful spirit, thanks to whom new passion
keeps this old heart alive so near the grave,
and who, besides help and happiness you gave,
single me out among these nobler folk;

    as once to sight, so now to soul you evoke
such comfort I forget the neglectful others,
my trust in you dispelling the *ifs* and *whethers*
of pain that no less than longing is my portion.

    And since this friend—true advocate (as I live!)—
has found you gracious, I'm grateful for your grace,
you too being burdened. So, these lines to you:

    It's unconscionable usury! to give
these dubious drawings—vile!—and in their place
be blessed with acquaintance beautiful and true.

80

I really believed, that first great day when, awed,
I saw your beauty entire and like no other's,
I could fix a loving eye (given my druthers)
on your least detail, as an eagle fronts the sun.

    No chance of that, as I saw soon, though—none:
who, without wings, can tail an angel? He
might as well sow seed on stone, strew loonishly
words on a gust of wind, match wits with God.

    Well then! if your blinding beauty that stuns me so
can't stand to have my poor old heart close by,
if in absence no trust, no care, much make-believing,

    what future's in store for me? What guide might go
alongside to help, direct me? Near you, I
burn at the stake. But afar—? It's death, your leaving.

In everything I see, the meaning's plain,
compelling me to love you, never leave you.
What isn't you is wrong for me, does harm.
Love, that all other wonders counts as vain,
tells me, for my soul's sake, I have to have you
—you, my sole sun—and thereby quite disarms
my other hopes, all objects of desire;
would have me live, afire
for you, or any like you, eyes the same,
eyelashes fine and curling almost so.
If too divergent, though,
(O eyes for which I live!) then there's no spark.
Heaven's only where you are; else, total dark.

82

Not even, in dreams sent soaring, can I imagine
a form, nude apparition or flesh and bone,
who'd so win over my will I'd dare disown
for such acquaintance the beauty I see in you.
    Still deep and deeper, without you, in the slough
of self I sink, till Love unmans me quite
of the vigor it gave. I try to set things right,
then nothing from Love but death threats. No compassion.
    Pelting off pell-mell from you's no use at all,
trying to double my distance from a handsome foe.
Can lagging limbs outrun spryer? At any rate
    Love dries, with his own hands too, the tears that fall,
promises to make precious every woe.
Nothing common here, nothing cheap, the expense so great.

83

What in your handsome face I see, my lord,
I'm hard put to find words for, here below.
Often it lofts my soul to God, although
wearing, that soul, the body like a shroud.

And if the stupid, balefully staring crowd
mocks others for feelings after its own fashion,
no matter. I'm no less thankful for a passion
pulsing with love—faith, honor in accord.

There's a Fountain of Mercy brought our souls to being
which all earth's beauty must in part resemble
(lesser things, less) for an eye alert to truth.

No other hint of heaven's here for our seeing,
hence, he that a love for you sets all a-tremble
already hovers in heaven, transcending death.

84

From ink, from pen in hand we see outflow
the several styles: high, low, and in-between;
so out of stone come noble forms or mean,
depending on how imaginative the art.

And, my dear lord, it's like that with your heart:
humility's there in equal parts with pride.
I only see what's most like me inside
that heart of yours. As smile or grimace shows.

One who's flung seed of grief, pain, woe abroad
(rain falls, itself and pure, but changes straight
in seedbeds to rank earth's variety),

he'll reap the same, by pain and sorrow gnawed.
Who eyes great beauty through a grief as great
sees only his suffering soul, racked with anxiety.

Having, my friend, your letter here in hand,
I scouted round and passed your howdy-do
to three high cardinals of that holy band.

To the Medicee-man who cures what's gone askew
I showed that same, and it brought such grand guffaws
his specs, on that nose of his, split right in two.

And the one you so respect, whose every cause
you second both here and there, seeing what you wrote
was tickled into uproarious applause.

The other who's "good at hush-hush" (and I quote)
for that Medicee the Less, I still can't track;
when he sees it, if he's a priest, you bet he'll gloat.

Plenty would swear off Christ to get you back
in Rome, and they'd be better off so; here
it's your heretics seem a less unholy pack.

Your letter's sure to alleviate, I've no fear,
the yearning most folks feel for you—if not
we'll let "the hangman" hustle them off the pier.

Old "Meathead," cured in salt so's not to rot
(he might be tasty toasted on a grill)
is mad for you; his own self he forgot.

And good old Michelangelo, who still
I think adores you, when he saw your screed
just hit the roof with jubilance. What a thrill!

He says the life his stonework effigied
won't make *your* name immortal, half as much
as your songs—and they're divine!—make him. Indeed,

he says no summer, winter dares to touch
your poems, that time and death, malevolent pair,
can't soil such merit with their dusty clutch.

As he, your friend and mine, said, well aware
how fine your verses are, "Some people tack
prayers onto kitschy saints, light candles there;

I'm like the schlock some good-for-nothing hack,

some dime-a-dozen Sunday painter slops
out of his pots to peddle by the stack.

    My thanks," he went on, "to Berni; that man cops
the prize at sizing *me* up. I'm not much.
They're really off the mark who think I'm tops.

    But his example, his instruction's such
its brilliance could work wonders, even make
a living man of a painted fake." This swatch

    of what he said, I give. For friendship's sake
him also I commend, as well I may.
I'm giving him this letter here to take.

    As line by line I wrote it, in dismay
I flushed a redder red—me writing *you!*
My writing's scribble-scrabble. You're distingué.

    Writer I'm not. My best respects, though, to
our mutual friend. Can't think of more right now,
except, come rain or shine, I'll prove true-blue.

    So very rare the preeminence you show,
you've won my love. Friar's robe or not, you'll see
I'll never fail you. Never ever! So

    I swear to that. And whatever I'd do for me,
for you I'd do even more. Now don't pooh-pooh
and don't let "Brother" bother. But feel free

    to ask, if there's ever anything. Up to you.

86

    Already burdened with a heavy heart,
I still thought I'd relieve the weight of woe
through tears and sobbing, or at least in part.

    But fate, abounding, filled to overflow
grief's source and stream, now welling unconfined
with another death—no worse pain here below!

    That death your own, dear father. Now in mind
two deaths, their claims distinct, for thought, talk, text:
fraternal, filial, separate though entwined.

My brother first, and you my father next;
to one my love, to one devotion's due.
And which the keener pain? My heart's perplexed.

    Memory paints one, still vivid to the view;
the other's sculptured live within me, which
more grieves me there, more stains my cheek. It's true

    there's solace yet: when one dies weathered, rich
in life's experience, less cause to lament;
mourning the young lifts grief to fever pitch.

    To suffering souls, death seems less cruelly sent
when it jibes with life expectancy, as read
by a mind the turbulent senses less torment.

    Who wouldn't mourn for a dear father dead,
seen lovingly, year by year, in youth, in age,
but never again, in the dim years ahead?

    Intensities of grief and woe we gauge
in different souls diversely; Lord, you know
how violently in me such feelings rage.

    My soul's not deaf to reason; even so
when overcome by grief, what's reason then?
The more I think, the more morose I go.

    And if the thought that grips me hadn't been
that a happy death means laughter high in heaven
at the very notion death can frighten men,

    my sorrow'd be far worse. I weep; there's leaven
for shrillest anguish in the certainty
one who lives well finds death his one safe haven.

    Our intellect, alas, is never free
from dementias of the flesh; just hearing then
their false appeal, the worse death seems to be.

    Sun dipped so many times—four score and ten!—
its shining torch beneath the sea, before
heaven's peace absolved you from the world of men.

    Thank heaven you'll feel earth's misery no more!
But pity the death I'm living yet, down where
through you heaven cast me in life's tug of war.

Now you're divine and death is dead; no fear
of change in your way of life, your heart's desire;
even as I write, pale envy hovers near.

Fortune and time don't venture near the choir
you're blissful in; on earth they tend and till
contentment's dubious rose; its deadly briar;

Your serenity no thundercloud can chill,
sequence of hours brings no compulsion, nor
have fate or chance a bearing on your will.

Your glory our blackest night can't overscore,
nor can our sun at noon show brighter sky,
not even when mid-July's aflame. And more,

your death has taught me my death: how to die,
dear father, whom in vision I behold,
though bonds of earth prevent my going so high.

But death's not worst of all (the things we're told!)
for one whose eve restores the primal day,
eternal, God be praised, on thrones of gold

where, through His grace, I trust you live, and pray
to see you up there, should my rational soul
rescue my frozen heart from ruts of clay.

If love of son and father, pure and whole,
increase in heaven, as all virtue does . . .

87

I wish I'd want what I don't want, Lord, at all.
Between this heart and Your fire an icy screen,
invisible, damps it down, so these routine
words falsify what I do; the pages lie.

Tongue says it loves You, but the heart's reply
is chilling: there's no love there. Nor can I know
which way to let grace enter, immerse it so
hard-hearted pride is hell-bent for a fall.

You be the one, Lord! Rend it! ramming through
closure that saw Your beauty dim and dwindle,
once light of the world's one sun, now cold as stone.

Send now the promised light that's one day due
to Your comely bride on earth! Oh then I'll kindle
the fire within, doubt-free, feeling You alone.

88

By a face of fiery cold, I'm set aflame
from a focus far away, itself like ice.
Two shapely arms hug me tight in a vice
like the Unmoved Mover's primal gravity.

A spirit like no other, made plain to me
only, itself undying, death to others;
heartwhole itself, it tangles me in tethers;
only doing good, undoes me just the same.

And how, signore, can a face so fair,
unfair to mine, with hot and cold torment it?
Your qualities? Yes. How flaunt them if they weren't?

Or, ravaging my happiness, that's where
it behaves like the sun itself (you'll not prevent it?)
bathing all the world in fire, itself unburnt.

89

Through your fine eyes I see such mellow light
as my own clouded ones could never see;
on your own feet I bear such weight with me
as my own laggard limbs aren't equal to.

Wingless myself, on yours I'm buoyant through
the skies; toward heaven itself your mind directs me;
I blush, go pale, as your sweet will affects me;
chilly in sunlight, scorched on winter nights.

My will is in your will as wheel in wheel;
your heart moulds every thought, my least one even;
my words, without your breath in them, expire.

Like the moon, lone rock in space, is how I feel
without you—the moon that none can see in heaven,
except where the sunlight touches—there it's fire.

I'm dearer to me, much more, than ever I was.
With you in my heart—pure treasure!—my worth grew,
as marble the sculptor gives a turn or two
brings more than the rough old stone it was. Just so

plain paper, inscribed or aquarelled, can grow
in appraisal; left blank, mere scraps we throw away.
I'm like that: chosen as target on the day
that incised in me—no pain!—your very face.

So marked, I'm a man immune wherever I go,
like one with a good-luck charm or sword in hand.
Before him all perils fade, their weapons brittle.

Spells against flood and fire, all these I know;
the blind have instant vision at my command,
and sovereign against all poison is my spittle.

91

So I can best endure
blazing intensity
when your eyes close and open brilliantly
to spare or scorch my soul,
your magnet eyes control
my soul, myself, my faculties. I'm sure
Love lags, quails, insecure
about dealing death because
he's blind as blind can be.
To pierce me through my poor
heart, now with yours, gives pause:
your breast he'd first transfix, not killing me
alone. Accordingly
he spares you, sparing me. The anguish then!
Deadly grief that means die, again, again;
alas, not dying when
I would have died, my heart being mine. I cry:
O give my own self back, so I can die.

92

Although time presses hard and prods us on
in escalating war
engaged in to restore
to earth our tortured, tired, and wandering limbs,
no truce with Love, who brims
with joy the heart, the soul with agony.
He locks, unlocks, alone,
that heart, won't spare me for
these last hours when the dim
and dubious other world looms over me;
ingrained iniquity
worries me, worse than ever now I'm old.
What tale crueller than mine ever was told?
Now time's too short to hustle woes away;
my heart burned, and was burned, so many a day
it's not itself. Cool reason spoke too late.
My heart, dead ashes in a rusty grate.

93

Should the senses' rapturous burning override
your handsome face, my lord, caught by some other,
they're impoverished, in a pother,
like cataracts raveling down the steep divide.
But the ardent heart, allied
to fire, the fiercer the better, can't accept
that the tears are rarer, less passionate the sighs.
The soul, that error spied,
and its longings for heaven kept
supreme, is glad the one, sent heavenward, dies.
Then reason must harmonize
in sense, heart, soul each dissonance; all four
agree that it's you, you always, they adore.

94

Kindly to others, to itself unkind,
a poor thing's born that peels away its skin
in pain to glove another. And therein
its only worth; we could say: born to die.

To clothe my living lord, how I wish I
could flay my dying hide to drape his shoulders,
so that, as snakes slough off their scurf on boulders,
I'd wake in death to a higher kind of life.

If only it came from me, that plushy pelt
that weaves itself into fabric for such dress
as that now hugging his handsome breast—for so

I'd hold him the whole day long; or else as felt-
soled footwear of pure silk I'd do no less
than bolster him through at least two winters' snow.

95

Give back to my eyes their flow, O spring, O river,
that welled from a source not yours, though strong and steady;
it left you broader, deeper, its surge and eddy
an impetus far more powerful than your own.

And you, air, burdened with my many a groan,
air shading our mournful gaze from skies too keen,
restore to my heart those groans, make more serene,
I pray, to my human sight your cloudy cover.

Return to my feet each footstep, trodden sward;
let the grass grow green again, the way be smoother.
Once deaf, O Echo, give back my long lament.

Relinquish, heavenly eyes, each fond regard
that lingered. I'll save them till I love another,
since all that I feel from you is discontent.

With all my heart I love you; if not so,
may I turn ashes, like dry wood in fire;
may I lose my soul, if elsewhere set aglow.

And if enchantment kindles warm desire
for alien beauty in some other eyes,
then take your own away and I'll expire.

It's you alone I cherish, idolize;
if not, may hope die, spirits quail and dwindle,
though once in your love so steadfast, buoyant, wise . . .

97

With heart of sulphur, flesh of tinder too,
bones like kindling, over these a soul
with no direction, none, and no control,
panting toward each impulse, each loveliness,

limping, with vision dim, mind under stress
in a world of noose and snare, all laid for me,
no wonder one such as I flares instantly
at the first blithe fire by chance come into view.

If high art filters down from heaven to earth
through our human hands, so that nature bows to art
(nature: authority in its own estate),

and if I, all ear and eye for this since birth,
feel affinity for the thief who scorched my heart,
then the fault's His who foredoomed it: fire's my fate.

98

Why ease the tension of this wild desire
with tears and sighing and words woebegone,
if this heavy cloak of grief the heavens have drawn
around us all, won't loosen soon or late?

Why does the heart urge "Languish on" if fate
shows death ahead for all? So let my eyes

conclude their days in peace. No earthly prize
seduces like love's agonizing fire.

But if the blow I sought myself, by sleight,
falls so I can't escape, my fate foreknown,
who's there, between grief and sweetness, meant for me?

If being bested and bound is my delight,
no wonder I'm made a prisoner, nude, alone,
as a cavalier in armor turns the key.

99

What a chance I had! I should have, while I could,
as Phoebus bathed the hill in his golden glow,
been lifted upon his wings, left earth below
and sought, beyond death, new glory in the sky.

But now he's gone, and all that hope put by
that he'd slow to a halt the flight of joyous days;
good reason my cold and guilty heart's a-daze:
grace turned thumbs down; heaven clanged its gate for good.

His wings were upward winds; his hill a stair,
Phoebus "a lamp unto my feet"; death's door
showed a marvellous and miraculous Beulah-land.

Without these, now, what hope death takes me there,
or what hope I've a heart such memories can restore?
Too late, the harm all done. Who'll take my hand?

100

When heaven confirmed your brilliance, most of all,
it was kind to your two eyes, but cruel to me,
as in its circlings through eternity
us it gave radiance, you the wings to soar.

Fortunate bird, your privilege so much more
than ours! seeing Phoebus and his glorious face;
and beyond that heavenly vision, given the grace
to fly by the hill of my calamitous fall.

101

The night prevails where Phoebus—that's our sun—
can't reach his shining arms all round our cold
and watery globe, too burly to enfold.
What's outside his embrace, we call "the night."

    A fidgety thing the night is; if we light
a little wick, she's stricken, good as dead;
she's given to hysteria—the least shred
of tinder lit by flint and she's undone.

    If we can say she's anything at all,
let's say she's daughter of both earth and sun:
shuns sun, but cuddles earth, whose shoulders shade her.

    Be what she may, to tout her's wrong. I'd call
her a widow, glum, suspicious—she's the one
fears her least foe, the firefly, as invader.

102

O night, comforting night, dark though you are,
to peace converting all effort at the close,
who glorifies you—ah, that one sees! He knows!
Right-minded too is the one who'll rightly prize

    your worth. You come; lackluster boredom shies
away. Calm hours and dewy dusk take over.
From the depths I'm drawn up, up—often to hover
in dream on the hoped-for heights, sad earth afar.

    O shadow of death itself, clapping the door
shut on all anguish harrowing heart and soul,
of remedies for our grievance, last and best,

    you doctor our fevered flesh to health once more,
and, drying our tears, remitting toil, you lull
the good man's tussle and tedium to rest.

Every shut-in room or space, every covered one,
whatever a wall of matter closes round
preserves the dark of night (though daylight's found
some inches off) from the sun's too glitzy glare.

It's true the dark's upset by flame or flare,
routed by sunbursts rending its serenity;
far tinier things make light of its divinity:
say a glowworm winks—a bug!—and it's undone.

What lies uncanopied, heaven heats: the swarm
of seed and seedling, myriad in the clay
plowmen have at, with mattock, hoe and harrow.

Mankind, though, is sown by night; his nobler form
is proof that the dark's far holier than the day,
as man is beyond the worth of field and furrow.

104

The One Who made, and from utter nothing too,
time, nonexistent till there's someone there,
divided the one in two, hung sun in air
for the one; for the other, nearer earth, the moon.

Fortune, chance, destiny—the three came soon
out of the two, for every person born.
The night was mine, the dark time; fate had sworn
from my look at birth, in cradle, that's my due.

And like the one who'll plagiarize his nature,
soul growing glummer with night's darkening gloom,
I grieve for my dismal days, so little worth.

But I think of you, then the sun, effulgent creature,
turns black of midnight to cerulean noon.
Your sign, the sun; your angelic friend from birth.

My gaze saw no mere mortal on the day
I found in your fine eyes quiet like none
on earth, so pure I saw therein the One
who storms my soul with love—a soul like its own.

And weren't my spirit drawn from God's alone,
earth's outward beauty had left it so aglow
that it longed for nothing. Mirage, all that! And so
it soared to the universal form straightway.

When one lives—truly lives!—his will won't mesh
with mortality; nor are things eternal cast
in the mould of time. For skin and bone, no haven.

Untamed desire's not love, just a flush of flesh,
and it kills the soul. Our honest love makes fast
friendships on earth. Death, faster though, in heaven.

106

From heaven it ventured forth, there must return,
the immortal soul. To your flesh, its lifetime jail,
an angel of mercy it came, to countervail
our tainted thought, show fit respect for earth.

My love's aflame only for this, whose worth
is beyond your classic beauty that takes the eye.
For what else, in this spawning hubbub born to die,
can a love all truth and honor hope to yearn?

That's how with all things noble, new-created,
that nature lavished her care on, heaven too
rifled its treasures for. Thanks be, that where

in the main God shows His glory, it's radiated
veiled in some mortal form it shimmers through.
And it's such I love, for the beauty mirrored there.

Drawn to each lovely thing, my doting eyes.
Drawn to its heavenly destiny, my soul.
Both with the one same goal,
no way, but in treasuring loveliness, to rise.
Stars in the highest skies
shower radiance from above;
toward those our longing flies:
earth calls the impulse "love."
Nothing true hearts can have
so kindles them with love, pilots them right,
as a face where eyes see plain the heavens' own light.

108

No rest here for the wicked, as folk say;
no grace or pardon for my grievous wrong.
Hardly, as I believed, my lucky day,
losing me, choosing you—the lure so strong.
Hope for rebirth in sun? The phoenix may;
no such return for me; life's not that long.
In loss, though, my delight; easy to see
the less I'm mine, more yours, the more I'm me.

109

Not always so prized and cherished by us all
is sensual bliss, that not
a one of us can spot,
beyond joy on the lip, its core of ash and gall.
So very rare, good sense,
to the mass it fades away,
but, scorned, on itself it happily relies.
So I, by the times outpaced,
learn hidden mysteries they
ignore, their poor soul slighted as it sighs.

Blind world! with your praise, ranks, honors all a prize
lavished on those to whom they least pertain.
Like a biting lash, the awareness! And the pain!

110

I'm here to say you've given earth your all,
body and soul and ranging mind together;
this coffin's the gloomy home in which you'll crawl.

111

My lady, if it's true
that you, so divinely beautiful, although
lodged with us here below
can eat, sleep, talk, communing as we do,
then not to follow you,
your truth by your courtesy avouched, what kind
of penalty for such sin can justice find?
A fellow plunged into
his broodings, or stone-blind,
is, of himself, in love a sluggard. Do,
dear lady, construe me true,
as I on any blankness, space to spare,
paper or stone, draw what I wish were there.

112

For a safe haven, for escape at last,
what's best to count on, promising no less
than prayer and weeping, they themselves in vain?
Now love and cruelty are encamping fast
around me, the one to kill me, one to bless,
this that would do me in, and that, sustain.
So fought for, I dare not die,
though in that death visions of comfort lie.
How many a time I'd flee

to heaven's eternal home wherein I'll see
beauty that's more than a proud lady's grace.
But then the one true face
I love and live for glows within my heart
and—Love, you've won! Death, beaten, slinks apart.

113

No slightest chance on earth her heavenly eyes
could ever exult in mine as I in hers.
With tears my vision blurs,
sorry return for the loveliness that plays
about her. O lovers, befooled so all your days!
How can her infinite beauty, her soul aglow,
differ from mine as if poles apart, and how
be so remote, that now,
both burning in love, her fire burns lax and low?
Love, straining between two souls contrasting so,
goes lame, in vexation hobbling off apart
from my true simple heart,
yet melts with reluctant pity all the same,
in tears departing, having come as flame.

114

Easily you confound
all hardness with your gaze, all brilliance too.
If ever a joy could kill, death's overdue
now I've discerned in you
such loveliness, but with greater goodness crowned.
And hadn't my soul been bound
so long in love's fierce fire, I'd have dropped down dead
when my eyes first read in yours the allurement there,
toward which they couldn't spare,
traitors to me, to incline wherever you led,
nor could I long be sad

—excusing you—that I'd not again be minded
to die. O beauty, with grace more boundless still,
your least show of goodwill
is a gift that can't *not* kill,
and not *not* leave those your eye finds less than blinded.

115

Wiles, guiles, smiles, gold and pearls, her gala ways—
on these who'd fix his gaze,
these worldly gauds, and not her heavenly glow
in which gold, silver show
her soul's own glory mirrored doubly bright?
No jewel with its own light
is a-dazzle; all's refulgence from her eyes.

116

I wouldn't if I could, Love, check the urge
(even as your furies surge)
to confide, yes, even swear
that your frown, your stony stare
invigorate all the more my soul to good;
and if sometimes you should
reprieve my doom, my anguished tears and sighs
as of one breathing his last,
I feel my heart, downcast,
fail with that fire whose torment glorifies.
O glow in heavenly eyes,
I treasure what speck of grace within me burns.
Chalk it as gain, though, when the loser learns.

117

If right desire takes wing
from any lovely thing
in flight to our God above,

why then my ladylove
alone is what eyes like mine are treasuring.
Oblivious of the rest,
for her alone I care.
Her alone—no surprise!—
I cry for, sigh for, die for. This love depends
on no merit I possess—
no, the soul finds comfort where
eyes mirror the very eyes
from whose heavenly glory every soul descends.
If the soul knows its last end
in that primal love, then it honors her here. Who
adores the lord loves the chatelaine there too.

118

Although my heart had often been aflame
with love till age blew in with icy breath,
this latest torture came
deadly as ever, with no hope but death.
For so my longing soul
on fiery coals would see its last of days
become its first within high heaven's choir.
No cove, no blackest hole
to hide in. Nothing stays
my death, except my dying, flayed in fire.
No power on earth to faze
death except death. On other hope relying,
that's death on death for one who lives by dying.

119

From the first whimper to the expiring sigh
now closer every day,
was any abused in so brutal a way
as I by this glamorous and savage star?

Unjust? Malign? That far
I'd never go, though best
if scorn had sooner crushed my love. Obsessed,
the more I gaze, my eye
finds mercies that belie
a merciless soul—no feeling in that breast.
O longed for passion! Just
milksops with milky eye could break away.
I see too well. Each day
I'm thankful for, each moment, first and last,
I looked on her, held fast.
Then if I'm wrong, wrong's welcome. Wrong I choose,
if truth, in its shining armor, 's bound to lose.

120

   Time now good-byes were said
to passion's agony;
age and desire are scurvily combined;
the soul, though, deaf and blind
to death and destiny
(as, Love, you've understood,
who, while confronting death, bring *her* to mind,
even if your bow we find
unstrung and shattered there,
bits, pieces past repair)
prays only: heap such troubles on my head!
To say *yet isn't cured* implies *not dead.*

121

   Just as you cannot not be lovely here,
no way at all you'd not be gracious too;
so, being mine, then you
cannot be able not to quite undo me.
And so, your kindness to me
being fully equal to your loveliness,

your beauty's end, no less
than your concern's, brings near
my ardent heart's own doom.
But since souls can progress,
when free, to their own sphere
to enjoy the Lord, by whom
all bodies from the tomb
are made eternal for their peace or woe,
I pray my flesh, although
so homely, you'd see in heaven, as here on earth.
Fair face, devoted heart have equal worth.

122

   If fire, so quick to char,
burning me, leaves no scar,
it's not that fire's more feeble, I more sound,
that where I'm safely found
like the salamander, many another dies.
Who turned my peace to torment I don't know;
by you your beauty's glow,
by me my honest heart
was never made, and no,
not ours to bid us part.
A lord of loftier art
consigned my very life within your eyes;
if love you'd not misprize,
O pardon me, as I the grief I dread,
which, more than she that kills me, wants me dead.

123

   The more it seems I agonize, the more
when you read it in my face
your beauty takes on grace,
grows sweeter, so I've less pain to deplore.
Love, torturing me before,

proves courteous, if you are
made lovelier by my pain.
If then your spirits soar,
my barbarous cruel star,
suppose the rumor reached you I lay slain?
Yet, if the fact is plain
that your beauty blooms with my every anguished breath,
then, withering, at my death
no glimmer of your glamor could remain.
Stay beautiful then! Deign
to let me live in this afflicted state;
since when I droop you're at your loveliest,
my soul's the more at rest.
Great pleasure counterweighs anguish as great.

124

My lady is so impetuous, devil-may-care,
that, as her glances kill, they lavish too
promise of joy and pleasure: as they do
she, sinking the dagger deeper, twists it there.
So that contrarious pair
thrill in my soul a moment, life and death,
brief as my one caught breath.
But mercy, though, to spare
anguish for trials more tense, gives it reprieval.
Good does less good than evil can do evil.

125

Such wealth of promise lies
in a lady kind and fair
that even seeing her there
I could feel as once I did—though old and slow.
Since death's cold jealous eyes
interpose everywhere

between my sad gaze and her own soft glow,
my yearning flame burns low
except when briefly I'm mindless of his glare;
but when my dour despair
shows him in his old place, then in a trice
my blither fire chokes under grinding ice.

126

    If the soul, in truth, from body once set free,
is dressed in flesh anew
and to these brief and few
days of our life and death comes back to be
this lady that I see
so beautiful today,
will she be, on returning, rigorous yet?
If reason's truthful, she
on arising will portray
one full of grace, a heart no rancors fret.
If she once closed in clay
her lovely eyes we'll see the awakening of,
knowing death, she'll pity me, who die for love.

127

    Not death so much, but its terror rescues me,
stepping in to help me flee
from a lady—fair, unfair!—who kills on sight.
When flames leap live and bright
from the fire I've leapt into through wild desire,
no way it won't be my pyre,
except for that death's-head in my house of clay:
when death's around, Love scents it, shies away.

128

The fear of death! Who'd shove
it off, or take to his heels
in flight, whatever its source, should let it lie.
Then, cruel and violent, Love
could plan more savage trials
to smite the adoring lover hip and thigh.
But since the spirit wants
—thanks be to death and grace!—a happier future,
who cannot *not* die cherishes that fear
more dreadful than the rest.
When a lofty lady flaunts
charms rare and strange, no creature
has a refuge half so dear
against her scorn or enslaving mercy. Just
when I weep and plead, her peal of laughter chills me.
I've only one hope then. That someone kills me.

129

By light more brilliant of a star more bright
the night sky kindles its twinklings from afar;
things less bright than you are,
nearby too, show you in your loveliest light.
Which way—this, that way—might
set your cold heart aglow
so he who burns isn't frozen by your tongue?
Plain folk by contrast show
your beauty tall and svelte,
face, dazzling eye, gold hair to shoulder swung.
You do your beauty wrong
in shunning folk like me;
best from amid a throng
shows your supremacy.
If you'd restore, lady,
what heaven must mulct from us to exalt you there,
we'd be far handsomer for it; you less fair.

130

No doubt much peril lies
in features as divine
as yours for a soul like mine,
near death, whose cold breath on my nape I feel.
I urge myself, "Be wise!"
would arm me, before death, in reason's steel.
But kindly as you deal
with me, who hear time toll,
you can't return my soul:
no doom so dour I'd shun your graciousness;
no day discard what many a season blessed.

131

From beneath two arching brows
Love still can re-arouse
live sparks at an age stone-cold to his wings and bow.
In beauty like that my feasting eyes carouse
till my fond soul allows
dart after dart to inflict cruel blow on blow.
Yet I'm abashed to know
that with the sweet an acrimonious breath
of shame comes, even of death;
not that Love yields to threats of loss or pain:
one hour's no match for what all my life engrained.

132

Whenever my past unrolls before these eyes
—hourly it does so!—then,
O fraudulent world, it strikes me yet again
what folly, what wrack in human nature lies:
hearts that have come to prize
your empty pleasure, your flattering caress,
stockpile the soul with overloads of woe.
Who experience it know

how often you profess
to lavish the peace and happiness you still
don't have—no, never will.
Long life, less grace; more roguery to repent;
short life, less load; soul lightsome for the ascent.

133

Life's final hours: brought there by many a year,
I know—late, late, O world!—your vain delights;
you offer peace you don't possess, false rights
to the lost repose before our birth down here.
The sense of shame, the fear
of time that heaven's law
foredooms, only bring back
the fool's paradise, once dear,
from which if one can't withdraw
he destroys the soul, leaves the body faint and slack.
I say, having known earth's rack
of anguish: in heaven he has it best of all
whose birthclout's closest to his funeral pall.

134

O blessed souls, who high in heaven delight
in remembered tears earth took no reckoning of,
are you still plagued by love,
or was that abandoned for your heavenward flight?
"Serene forever, quite
beyond all time, we're free
of envy in our love, of tortured sighing."
I'm bound for misery,
if such the lover's plight:
it's love and serve and suffer—no denying.
If lovers are relying
on heaven as friend, not earth,

why was I given birth,
made just for love? To live long? Bitter blow!
Short life's too long for true hearts goaded so.

135

    With much of time and life gone, all the more
this love beats in the door;
leaves me no moment free
as I'd imagined in the remote past.
Poor soul, you writhe and roar
like one doomed wrongfully,
for me and your own perdition struck aghast.
Love, death—between them cast,
the deception and the dread!—I'm so in doubt
that when I've puzzled out
what's better, lo! I seize upon what's worse.
Good counsel bows; bad habits are my curse.

136

    Flooded, the soul pours out
its tears from deep within,
lest welling springs begin
to quench the very fire they bring about.
No other help, no drought
avails: my endless weeping
revives me, old and slow, in flames you raise.
Harsh, hostile, yes—but fate's not so without
some kindness in its keeping
it won't chafe less the more my soul's ablaze.
So your heartwarming gaze
within—though weeping outwardly—I cherish,
exultant to survive where others perish.

If, to rejoice, you crave our tears and woe,
the crueller then your arrows, Love, the dearer;
that way the wound is nearer
to death; no space between, no time to languish.
To murder lovers so
means no more tears for you, for us less anguish.
So my thanks only go
to you for death, and not for torture. They
best cure all ills who take our life away.

138

Humbly I bow my shoulders, bear the yoke;
shake off, with just a smile, fate's bitter blow;
to her, my best-loved foe,
I give a faithful heart with love alight.
No torture makes me quake;
my only fear, that none can test me quite.
If, so serenely bright,
her face makes pain the food on which I thrive,
how can pain kill? Instead, it keeps alive.

139

In lovelier and crueller flesh than yours,
there never lived and breathed,
lady, another lady half so fair.
Your hauteur, since it slurs
that beauty, predicts a surer hell beneath
our feet than my sufferings do a heaven up there.
I don't hide, but don't care
to say if, yes or no, I'd share your sin
to be with you, if not here, in hell when dead,
or, if you change, and I through anguish win
salvation, you'll be my heavenly peace instead.
With you, if sweet being in

that hell, imagine what our heaven could be!
O doubly blessed me!
Two to adore, amid minstrelsy above:
my God in heaven, and my earthly love.

140

If the soul returns, that last
of hours, to the body it loved and longed for so,
to be saved or damned on Judgment Day (it's said)
then in hell there'd be less woe
wherever your beauty cast
its spell to delight a while the dreary dead.
Or if bound for heaven instead
—and to join you on that flight
is the goal that, heart and soul, I'm yearning for—
God might yield less delight,
if all other joys by right
gave way, as here, to your charm. You I'll adore
hereafter, whether more
a gain in your cheering hell's sad unforgiven,
or a loss in your casting a moment's pall on heaven.

141

If I'm to believe my eyes now, your response
to my hopes, dear lady, is casual and brief.
Making do, I've some relief
contemplating the radiant prospect of your eyes.
Though a cold reception daunts,
it doesn't mean supreme beauty can't surprise
with joy. So if I surmise
you've reactions within at odds with your soft glance,
it's not certainty—no chance!—
I look for, nor perfect joy (as once in youth):
better nurse a delicious doubt than gag on truth.

142

I think it may be, so
the old fire just won't die
in the chilly season when so little's green,
Love abruptly bent his bow,
and he had good reason why:
in a sensitive heart no arrow won't hit clean.
Then those wintry fields regreen
for a lovely face, and my fresher wound's the worst,
his last arrow deadlier always than the first.

143

Life's quick and brief; the more my days fly by
of what little now remains,
a ring of fire enchains
me more and more in my loss and misery.
Time nags; heaven, hurried, is no ally
against what, all these years, I've made of me,
and since you refuse to see
that your fire's more than enough,
fire in which rocks are worn to shapeless grit,
and the heart fares worse. Thanks be,
O Love, that the one less tough,
less invincible, chars to ashes bit by bit.
For me, though, fortune's pit
is a stroke of luck: your warring ways I dread,
but they do me in: you're gentler to the dead.

144

At times I project ahead
conceptions truly grand
that I swear to take in hand
some day—which may never come. Vain, stupid scheme!
For when death hangs overhead
my present shrivels; my future's but a dream.

And that lovely face I seem
on fire for! But I hope to heal, hope even to bloom
so I'll live on, those long years in the tomb.

145

If she rejoices in my tears, and you
live on them, Love, while I'm still forced to feed
my days on grief—indeed
I dine on ice from many a bitter floe—
then were she good she'd give
us two a death from too much kindness; so
better is worse. We know
diets reversed reverse their consequence:
she'd lose her joy, and we our lives, we two;
so, Love, at the expense
of life itself your promised help's in view.
To a soul numbed through and through,
better to have for years life's rasping breath
than a lady's favor, hand in glove with death.

146

Looks thrown away on others
from me are stolen, though
I wouldn't call it theft; they're yours to give.
But if your eyes' come-hithers
for clods and riffraff glow,
and not for me—I'm done for! I can't live.
Would you, Love, dare forgive
when fools are given free
this beauty she denies
to truer souls that prize
your own high courtesy?
Love, change her! Let her be
of a kinder heart, with looks that make one gag,
and then fall in love with me—the pathetic hag!

Please tell me, Love, if that lady had a soul
merciful as her face is lovely, who
(if their wits weren't jogged askew)
wouldn't gladly surrender all to her, part and whole?
In my case, how could it be
I'd have better served and loved her, were love returned,
when, though despised and spurned,
I loved her more than I would had she loved me?
    "By the gods above, you men! Now can't you see
best to take whatever comes? If she misbehaves
when you're stowed in the grave,
revenge for the pain she gave
you'll get in full, and for insults by the score,
for then it's you she'll love, as you love her now.
Too bad you've so long a wait to learn just how
I'll comfort you for the injuries you bore.
Consider, though, once more:
A heart proud, generous, pure, made little of,
responds not with pardon only, but with love."

148

I'd feel the more secure,
my lady, with lesser favor—a lesser threat
to my life, doublet less wet
with tears from the twin rivulets of my eyes.
Too great a favor's likely to obscure,
no, even annul what merit in me lies.
A man who's truly wise,
not magnifying his own stature,
deals with no pleasure not within his power;
too much can paralyze;
a modest creature
of modest fortune lives quietly, hour by hour.

Your sweetest gift my palate takes as sour:
who'd give his heart to one whose hopes are nil,
likely gives death. Joy's angina can kill.

149

    I'll surely be thought a dullard in talent, art
by one who, I'm afraid,
with overgenerous aid
kills me. Less mercy had accomplished more.
But my soul shrank off apart,
like an eye one source is all too brilliant for.
I saw it hover, soar
into wholly impossible skies where it couldn't take me,
nor I equal her slightest gift in any case,
so lofty, serene she is. That thought should make me
know that at best I show a thankless face
to this lady, full of grace
so abundant it kindles others with the same.
A raging fire burns less than a focused flame.

150

    Great mercy, my lady, as likely as great pain
can kill a robber whose execution pends;
blood in his veins gone icy, there he stands
drained of all hope—then the stunning jolt: "You're free."
    So with such grace as yours, a rarity
in this wretched life of mine, grief crowding grief.
Here's mercy in superabundance! The sweet relief
could be more of a threat to life than anguish can.
    News good or bad, if poignant enough, can kill
on the spot, contrary as the two may be;
one bursts, one cramps the heart—same fate ensuing.
    So if your beauty, which Love and heaven bred, still
would have me live, play down my ecstasy.
Great gifts are often the fragile soul's undoing.

Nothing the best of artists can conceive
but lies, potential, in a block of stone,
superfluous matter round it. The hand alone
secures it that has intelligence for guide.

The peril I'm running from, the good descried
in you, proud lovely lady—yes, heaven's own!—
are virtual in yourself. I'm doomed, I groan:
art thwarting the very end it longs to have.
Not love, then, and not your beauty, your famous name,
disdain or marble mien, fate high or low,
is the cause I languish long here, hold my breath.

If mercy and death in your heart attend, then blame
my feeble wit: though the two affect me so,
it can realize the one only. And that's death.

152

As by subtracting, my lady, one creates
from rugged mountain stone
an image of flesh and bone
developing even as the stone grows less,
so my soul's better traits
quiver beneath the excess
of the burdensome cadaver's gloomy weight,
like a rough shaggy husk around it grown—
hidden traits that you alone
could deliver—in my state
now I've neither grit nor gumption of my own.

153

A mould's not alone in this:
empty of work within, it waits to hold
silver or molten gold
it can form—but must be shattered to let go.

With the glow of love, I'm so:
it fills the immense abyss
of my wish for an infinite beauty, for her sake,
my adored one, source of bliss
to my heart and soul on the slippery roads I take.
Her welcome nobleness
through such fine eyelets into my void descends,
if she leaves me, it's through shattered odds and ends.

154

My lady, you raise me so
high above me, there's no way
—I won't merely say, to *say*—
but even conceive it, since I'm me no more.
Why not more often soar,
since I may, on the wings you lend,
where I'd hover high round the beauty of your face?
Why let such orbits end,
since there's nothing heaven wants more
than our rising, flesh and all, to Paradise?
Except though: it never dies,
my soul, if, through you, itself and I part ways.
Then my soul's in heaven with you. O blessed days!

155

Your kindness to me, and the ways of fate,
each taking a different turn,
mean, lady, I must learn
between sweet and bitter how to arbitrate.
To my burning wish your great
concern and mercy show,
just as your outward beauty takes the eye.
But foul fortune, of late
our pleasure's dogged foe,
taunt after taunt has newer sleights to try.

Suppose though it put the ancient rancors by,
bowing to my desires
—why, then your mercy tires!
Between my tears and laughter, worlds apart,
no midway passage to ease the troubled heart.

156

That whole way up to your brilliant diadem
by a climb so long and sheer,
my lady, there's none comes near,
unless courteous condescension figure too.
As the rough routes up get steeper, scaling them
I grow faint, am out of breath—and just halfway.
But thoughts of your beauty stay
before me—so heavenly!—giving pleasure yet
to a heart athirst for all things high and rare.
But so I may cherish your loveliness, I pray
come lower where I can set
fond eyes on you. In this thought I'm less forlorn:
maybe your clairvoyant scorn
that I love what's low but love less what's on high
is excusing you for the sin I sinned thereby.

157

Your merciful, sweet care
and with it, my lady, *you*
my vital spirits drew
from my heart to my outer body everywhere.
And so the soul, balked there
of a course by nature laid,
in that sudden storm of joy forsakes me quite.
As cruelly you prepare
to leave me (fatal aid!),
those spirits throng to the heart in huddled flight.
But, your return in sight,
I feel them rushing from the heart again.

Both ways torment me then:
being helped, being hurt—both deadly. But we've seen
who greatly love find worse: being in between.

158

It seems, Love, out you've flung
all thought of death; but such
a favor lames too much
the soul itself, that was happier before.
Fallen the fruit, skin shriveling more and more;
what once was sweet, now bitter on the tongue.
Worse torment to deplore
as the waning days rush by:
infinite pleasure amid hours too brief.
Mercy come late, therefore,
can only terrify,
so mighty, it's death to flesh, joy's ruin too.
Yet, profound thanks to you
now I'm old: if it means that here's my way to die,
not death, but your mercy glories where I lie.

159

To be less unworthy, my exalted lady,
of that gift, your wondrous courtesy when we met,
I tried, with all my heart, to repay the debt
with some token of the little wit God gave me.
    But saw no way at all—no, not to save me!—
couldn't climb that high with the energies I muster.
Pardon me then. I was rash to try. Mere bluster.
I lapsed and learned, so am less a fool already.
    How far from truth's straight path has he gone afield
who'd imagine the rain of grace from your heavenly urn
could be matched by my poor trinkets, frail and shoddy.
    Talent and art and all remembrance yield;
for treasure from heaven no mortal makes return,
though a thousand times he try. Not anybody.

160

If obligated by so great a favor
as, at death's door, to have one's life restored,
for such support, what imaginable reward
would absolve the debtor from his obligation?

And were there any, then wouldn't the sensation
of infinite mercy be taken more for granted?
Love lose its sovereignty? Its value scanted
if the person saved could recompense the savior?

Hence, my lady, to let your benevolence shine high
above me as you yourself, I long to nurse
not courtesy but ingratitude. In reality

if better and worse on one dead level lie,
then the one I love's no more my lord. Of course:
no place for a lord in a climate of equality.

161

What file's incessant bite
left this old hide so shrunken, frayed away,
my poor sick soul? When is it due, the day
that sloughs it off, and heaven receives you, where
in primal joy and light
you lived, unvexed by the perilous flesh you wear?
Though I change hide and hair
with little life ahead,
no way to change behavior long engrained,
cramping me all the more as years go by.
I'm envious, Love, I swear
(why hide it?) of the dead,
a panicky muddle-head,
my soul in terror of its sensual tie.
Lord, as the last hours fly,
stretch out in mercy your two arms; make me
less what I've been, more what you'd have me be.

162

Now on the left foot shuffling, now the right
in search of my salvation, I'm astray.
Vice? Virtue? Caught midway,
my heart's confused; these trouble and exhaust me,
as, when dark clouds benight
all heaven, paths seem to intertwine; they've lost me.
Here's the blank page I lay
before your sacred ink;
love, cease to spellbind; mercy, tell things true,
so that the free soul may
not let life's tag end sink
in folly's bog. Love, clear my eyes anew.
O high divine one, you
tell me, does heaven look down on humbled sin?
Superior virtue is more welcome in?

163

Hating myself, the more I run away,
my lady, from me, the more toward you I'm thrust;
my soul then, as it must,
quakes for me less there, where it hopes I'll stay.
What heaven provides, I pray
to realize in your face
and lovely gaze, where all redemption lies,
for well I know, each day
scanning others, there's no trace
of virtue unless the heart shows in the eyes.
So rare such loveliness!
To see it's my single craving, pure and whole.
Rare glimpses, though, are like Lethe to the soul.

For a reliable guide in my vocation
beauty was set before me as birthright,
a mirror and a lamp for either art.
To see it differently's without foundation.
This only can lift our vision to that height
where both my painting and my sculpture start.
    Even though the ignorant and lurching mind
thinks beauty—which stirs the heart and lifts to heaven
every healthy soul—is sensual at base,
sick eyes can't move from earthly to divine,
but are bogged down here forever, with not even
a chance to ascend—vain thought!—except by grace.

165

If we constrain the eyes' easy response
by overuse, wits fail,
uneasy fears prevail.
When one's too self-assured, he'd best beware:
deluded, he'd ensconce
as loveliest what at best is middling fair.
Now, my lady, I can swear
no mere complacent habit bound me there.
How could it, when so briefly our eyes met,
yours cloistered, and mine yearning that way, lonely.
Just one sole moment set
my heart afire. I saw you one time only.

166

My lady, these eyes see vividly—far, near—
your radiant face, wherever it is—here, there.
Where eyes can go, however, our feet forbear,
forbidden to bring hands, arms to rendezvous.
    The soul, intelligence uncorrupt and true,
can, thanks to the eye, aspire to your beauty's height,

since free to fly, not flesh-bound. No such flight
is permitted, even for love, to bodies here.
Our bodies, so mortal, cloddish, without wings,
can't follow the least of angels in their zone.
Eyes, only, exult and revel in all they do.
Lady, if you've such power in celestial things
as here on earth, make all of me eye alone,
all eye, to delight, the whole of me, in you.

167

From where you triumphed in me, Love, right here,
naked—forget the bow, the arrows drawn—
death drives you out with grimace of disdain,
his shrouds of ice encrusting your once dear
hearthfire, its little heyday quickly gone.
In every valiant heart death has domain,
not you, Love; winged in vain
you fluttered round me, but turn tail today.
Green days disgust us when we're old and grey.

168

Because there's half of me which, heaven-born,
is longing always for its homeward flight,
my being bound so tight
by her peerless beauty that I burn and freeze
means I've a spirit torn:
parts so contrary each rob each outright
of the good I'd have were my soul intact, at ease.
If any time, though, she's
to change her ways, so half of me's without
its heaven, but in her friendly graces—oh,
my thoughts, bleak, blown about,
would cluster round her joyfully, even though
heaven doomed my soul below;
while she's inclined, I'd be—that hope's my goal!—
not halfway hers—no, wholly! heart and soul!

Impassioned as I am,
she makes a fool of me,
kind outside—but that savage heart of stone!
I told you, Love, flimflam
was all we'd ever see.
Want things from others, and you lose your own.
Drop dead's her wish. I've sown;
I reap. The pain's my fault. The moral, viz:
Being believed's no sin. Believing is.

170

Great beauty scattering its brilliant flame
sets a thousand hearts aglow;
many hands heave to and fro
a weight that would be their death, one at a time.
Confined fire calcines lime
from a boulder hard as steel
(anyone with half an eye in his head would know),
grit that in water soon dissolves away.
Such flames as thousands feel
for this divine one, play
about my heart in its inner sanctum. So
if my tears' constant flow
can dissolve a heart so hard, far better I
not exist than live in fire and never die.

171

Among the memory of all lovely things,
we've need of death, to take that face away
as he took its owner once, an earlier day.
Death, changing fire to ice, laughter to grieving,
such hate for beauty brings
that its triumph dies in the heart that he's bereaving.

With his least retrieving
of those beautiful eyes to where they stirred desire,
we'd be dry kindling in a raging fire.

172

She's made her mind up, the
wild woman none can tame:
I should burn, drop dead, my frame
shrink to a wizened pigmy's. That's her goal.
A vampire, she leaves me
bloodless, unmanned, unstrung, body and soul.
She pretties for her role
in her trusty mirror, where
as she prinks and preens, she croons to herself, "Divine!"
Turns my way; her eyes roll:
I'm old. In the mirror there
her face shows the more charming next to mine.
You ugly Florentine,
that's her thought? Lucky me, though. I've parlayed her
into something lovelier than nature made her.

173

If a joyous heart makes beautiful the face
and a glum one, ugly—what of her who's both
lovely and cruel, being loath
to return the fervent love I feel for her?
Because my eyes appraise,
thanks to my stars at birth,
among various beauties, those superior,
then all the worse for her
who makes me often say,
when I look downcast, it's my heart shows through.
As self's what we portray
when we paint madame (or try),
if we're kept on tenterhooks, is the likeness true?

For both, more pleasure's due
if I work away with a merry heart, eyes dry:
she's even more beautiful, and no homelier I.

174

From what these eyes, my lady, see of you
(what's in your heart is dark, beyond their scope)
my weary thoughts, I hope,
enjoy some moments of delicious rest.
Besides, a franker view
of what's within might leave me more distressed.
If cruelty can nest
in a heart whose warm concern
your beautiful eyes assure my suffering of,
right now the moment's best
(true lovers only yearn
for this) to show, as your eyes would, warmer love.
A cold heart's not above
overruling your eyes—but they're lovely yet! I still
revel even as you deceive me. Always will.

175

So, Love, it hasn't healed, not even the least
of wounds from your gilded arrows long ago;
and there's worse to come, I know,
forecasting, from long-gone troubles, what's ahead.
Against the old you've eased
your assault; I'm safe. Or must you fight the dead?
Add wings to your bow of old
to plague me, naked, lame;
make your coat of arms her eyes
that kill me quicker than your arrows do.
What stands me in good stead?
Nor shield nor armor holds;
only honor dignifies
defeat. But my pyre means infamy for you.

A weak old man—all too
tardy and slow this last escape I choose.
Victory's in flight. To grapple means to lose.

176

No need at all for your angel loveliness
to bind me (when bound already) with more rope.
If memory's as I hope,
what made me prisoner and prey was a glance from you.
Applied pain can so stress
the weakened heart that it soon succumbs. But who
could imagine what came true
for this rough old log, charred dry? No sooner seen
by your lustrous eyes than it turned to Maytime green.

177

Bright in our minds, but in the dark earth stranded
her celestial beauty lies. From death's foul blow
her good right arm had kept her safe. But no!
Why didn't it, poor girl? She was left-handed.

178

Her beauty's alive in heaven! I believe her
without a peer even there—forget vile earth!
(where she was called "Left-handed," half in mirth
by the common folk, too blind to fall adoring).
For you, just you, she was born; there's no restoring,
chisel on stone, her beauty, pen on paper.
Far more divine than art of mine could shape her
the image your memory treasures, charmed forever.
And if, the way our sun's too luminous for
all other stars, she dazzles every mind,
for you, so very close, she's all euphoria.
Now, for your peace, God makes her all the more
lovely, beyond your highest hope. We'll find
only God—God knows not I!—makes forms so glorious.

If his bright eyes are closed and laid to rest
here all too soon, by this we're comforted:
in life, concern for those was good as dead;
in death, concern's alive in many a breast.

180

My fervent prayer, if any pity me
now free from earth, though buried here below,
is: save your tears, down cheek and chest aflow,
for those still bound to chance and destiny.

181

"So tell me, Death, why not possess some face
already worn with age? Why mine instead?"
"Because long life, on earth's corruption fed,
deserves, in heaven's pure ambience, no place."

182

Death didn't wish to lay Cecchino low
the usual way, with weight of year on year,
but so, though here interred, he'd reappear
in heaven, his youthful glamor still aglow.

183

Such brightness, under earth now, put to shame
all other mortal beauty here below
that Death, whom kindly Nature hated so,
to curry favor with her, doused the flame.

184

My name meant "Arms." But little help to me
my arms when death came raging at me, "Die!"
Better to boast another name, more spry,
like "Foot." Named Foot, I might have footed free.

185

Born, died. Now bedded by the churchyard wall.
So cruel and instantaneous was death
that, leaving body breathless in a breath,
soul hardly knew it touched on earth at all.

186

No way he who undid me can restore
to those he impoverished of it, here on earth,
the wealth of beauty given me at birth,
if he means to endow me with it as before.

187

Inside, his soul could not be outside too
to admire, as we, its form now laid below.
Even finer home the soul expected, though,
in heaven than here on earth. And so withdrew.

188

If nature now deferred to death, dejected
when this fair face was stolen, none the less
revenge in heaven impends; it means to dress
the soul more royally when resurrected.

189

Closed now his shining eyes, that dazzled so
they made our purest, loveliest eyes go dim;
his though are now relit, since death took him.
Gain countering loss. Which weightier, who's to know?

190

Here I'm thought dead. Alive, I comforted
the world by being there. A thousand souls
played in my heart a thousand loving roles.
Now I'm but one soul less. That means I'm dead?

191

Souls rise alive from the body's sad last bed.
Mine too, though some thought life had ended quite.
If so, why fear my haunting you by night?
No way, were I now unquestionably dead.

192

If true (and it is) that with body's final breath
the soul, cut loose from flesh (which it only bore
because heaven imposed that chore),
breaks free, it feels only then supreme delight,
becoming divine in death
as sure as we're born, down here, with death in sight.
No sin in this; we're right
to change funeral woe to mirth
when we stand about to mourn the newly dead,
for the soul, escaping earth
and the frail remains, then, there, on the deathbed,
finds perfect peace instead.
Such their true friends desire, in equal measure
as pleasure in God transcends all earthly pleasure.

193

His beautiful eyes! I hardly saw them, only
open a while in this fleeting world we know
before they closed, his last day here below,
to open on beatitude, God's glory.
Death saw to this, not I: the unhappy story
too soon concluded. And too late I knew
the beauty of eyes whose memory stays with you,
but left my impassioned spirit cold and lonely.
And so, Luigi, to make that peerless form
of our Cecchino endure in stone forever,
now that they're earth in earth, the limbs we knew,

I'd need a model to keep my focus firm.
If two who love are transformed so each is other,
you pose. For it's all the same: carve him, carve you.

194

Too early fallen asleep here, I'm alive,
though fate says dead. I've moved; my lodging's new.
I'm living in your thoughts. You miss me too.
While love lives on in lovers, I survive.

195

"If two hours' dying steals a hundred years,
five years could cheat one of eternity."
"Not so. One day's a century if he
in a glance sees life entire. Then disappears."

196

O lucky me, to look upon me dead!
O generous heaven, not hoarding me for age!
What better gift than ordering me offstage,
to spare me the long catastrophe ahead?

197

My flesh turned earth, my bones turned naked shame,
without the lustrous eye, the engaging face,
confirm, for the one my gaiety and grace
bewitched: what a grisly cage our mortal frame!

198

If it could be, to revive my life once more,
your tears turned flesh and blood to array these bones,
that's a cruel kindness done me—to postpone
my heaven for grovelings on earth's mouldy floor.

III

199

Who grieve now at my grave, in vain they pray,
tears glittering down the grave's stone canopy,
to have me back, like fruit on a withered tree.
No chance of the dead arising tall in May.

200

Cold stone, none knows but you, my gaol forever,
that I was once alive. To some who saw
me then, it seems a dream. Death's greedy claw
cancels our every *Used to be* with *Never.*

201

From clutch of clock and calendar now fled,
my bondage once, I dread going back again
more than I shrank from death, not knowing then
die meant being born, meant death itself lay dead.

202

One of the Bracci, I. Now, as you see,
a portrait only. But I'm grateful, Death.
This painted me's in luck: though out of breath,
feted through gates that barred the living me.

203

A Bracci born. From birth, born wailing, I'd
seen little of the splendid sun. And yes,
I'm dead forever—wouldn't wish it less
since in my lover's heart I never died.

204

I'm dearer dead than ever I was, before
death stole me from my love. Although no longer
we pleasure each with each, his love's the stronger.
O generous Death, my thanks: being less I'm more.

205

If death has buried here, hardly in leaf,
earth's loveliest flower of all, its noblest too,
what's there more poignant even death could do?
No death at eighty so abounds in grief.

206

From heaven my beauty, flawless and divine.
From mortal father my mortal frame alone.
If God's own portion die, this skin and bone
into what sad detritus should decline?

207

I'm death's forever, who, that one forlorn
brief hour, was yours alone. What beauty though
and ecstasy came with me! But the flow
of grief ensuing! Better not been born.

208

Gone under now, the sun you loved to greet
and learned too soon to grieve. Day's mere beginning.
Others live on—less beautiful, less winning.
The duller they, the more death dragged his feet.

209

Why fallen so soon asleep? Not hard to tell:
to give heaven back myself in early bloom
for a role no other in heaven could assume,
for all earth's beauty her model nonpareil.

210

Peace, life—he found them in my open eyes.
Where now his life and peace that mine are shut?
In Beauty's eyes? They closed with mine. Where but
in Death, since there his prize possession lies?

211

If, while I lived, a someone, eyes on me,
found life more sweet, then now, my beauty dead,
such loss is torture to him. Worse though, dread
that another joins me sooner here than he.

212

No other handsome face such power possessed
to wound as this young Braccio, here interred.
Our best and brightest fell. Till, envy-stirred,
Death struck, "Enough! I'm left what's second-best."

213

Young Braccio's buried here. To mend a lack
in nature's treasury, God designed his features.
Pearls before swine! Quite lost on us poor creatures.
God gave us just a glimpse—then took him back.

214

His life gave yours rich reason for thanksgiving,
Cecchino's did, who lies here. They survive
at ease, who never saw him when alive.
Some saw him and still live? Don't call it living!

215

Ashes to ashes, spirit to the sky,
so fate ordains. Who love me all the same
in death preserve my beauty and fair fame;
this stone, the mortal swathing I put by.

216

Within this tomb our handsome Braccio's laid.
As body gets its form from soul alone,
so here his spirit glorifies cold stone.
A handsome scabbard for a handsome blade.

217

If Braccio's beauty, phoenix-like, could be
restored to life, he'd shame that fabled pyre
—resurgent after absence, bright as fire,
he'd dazzle all who first saw blinkingly.

218

The sun of Braccio's under earth. The sun
of nature too, obscured forever now.
No dagger did it, and no broadsword. How?
By the least wind a winter flower's undone.

219

A Bracci, I. Alive because I'm dead.
I, of all those on earth, am heaven's now.
No heaven's left, down on earth. Heaven won't allow
earth entry here. Great gates clang shut instead.

220

Cecchino here has laid his body low
in death—no nobler dust beneath the sun.
Rome weeps, but heaven's in ecstasy that one
soul—forget body!—is pure joy aglow.

221

Braccio lies here. No less a tomb could show
how great his worth, no rites less sanctified.
Lodged statelier than in life. Death, when he died,
paid honor in heaven above, on earth below.

222

Death stretched an arm, stole fruit not ripened yet.
Fruit? Blossom rather. Just a boy, fifteen.
Only his tomb, to hold him so, is seen
as jubilant. Eyes—the wide world through—are wet.

Mere mortal once. Divine, though, born to be.
Short time on earth, but heaven's forever mine.
Rapturous change! when even death's benign,
deadly to many, but new life to me.

224

Death shut those eyes, him too it shut below
and, freeing a soul no stain of earth defiled,
changed this life to that other—still a child!—
life the earth-grubbing old may never know.

225

A Bracci once. The soul in me withdrew,
leaving my beauty bones and grime. O grim
gravestone, don't dare gape wide again. Let him
who loved me treasure yet the form he knew.

226

The soul lives on, I know it, lying here,
dead though not dead—for life was truer death.
A Bracci, I. If soon run out of breath,
less need of pardon for life's curt career.

227

Braccio retrieves from earth the mortal scrim
that veiled his soul. Before the day of doom,
as mercy willed. Arising from the tomb
that day, he'd shame the rest. Less heaven for them.

228

Earth lends us flesh, heaven lends the soul, the two
loans long-term mostly. But young Braccio's dead!
What restitution's to be given instead
for all that beauty, all those decades due?

Be sure, my eyes, you know
quick time goes by and the dread hour draws near,
soon to forbid your grieving tears to fall.
May mercy spare you, though,
while my divine one's here,
deigning to live on earth with us at all.
If grace breach heaven's wall
for every blessed one,
and this my living sun
leaving us here, returns to heaven, then
what's left on earth you'd care to see again?

230

To see that your famous beauty still endures
on earth, but in one more bountiful, less stony,
why doesn't nature, without ceremony
snatching back glories doomed to fade in you,
    keep them, serene, angelic, to use anew
in a more gracious lady's form and face?
Why doesn't love lend a hand, conferring grace
and kindliness on a truer heart than yours?
    And why not garner too my many a sigh,
my torrent of tears, my yearnings all in vain,
reserving those for her new love's armory?
    Maybe, born later and luckier than I,
he could kindle her pity with my wasted pain,
and not bungle the favor never granted me.

231

Too late for Love to set my heart aflame,
or for mortal beauty to thrill or terrorize.
With life's end, stricken sighs
for wasted time when little's left. You've thrown,
Love, many a blow; your aim

death frustrates now; he eyes
me for more brutal batterings than I've known.
My plans, my words, windblown
by you to raging fires (myself their prey),
are changed to a torrent of tears;
with them—I pray God hears—
may all my heavy sins be washed away.

232

No differently the guilty wretch hangs back
than I, headed for death;
as justice ruled, his path
leads to the spot where soul and body part.
Like me then: on my track
waits death, but bides his time. Love's cruel of heart
even so; his devilish art
plaguing me hour by hour
with hazardous options, though I sleep or wake.
Hope's impotent; can't start
old fires, can only cower;
or else it sears me, though I'm old and grey.
What's better? Worse? Can't say.
I'm in terror of your glance, Love! There's my fate.
You kill the quicker when your coming's late.

233

If, vulnerable from early youth, a heart
too green is blighted by even a shy liking,
then what's the effect of a conflagration striking
late in life when it's callous—charred and hardened?
More cramped, one is, as time goes by, more burdened,
less room to live, be lively in, show worth.
Then what's the effect, near our last days on earth,
if abruptly, from love at play, new wildfires start?

Then what's the effect? Exactly as expected.
I'm ash in a searing wind, but all the same
clean: where there's flesh afire no maggots breed.
  If green I wept, by flickering wicks attracted,
now that I'm matchwood amid sheets of flame,
can my soul, in this body, hope to long abide?

234

  It's not enough, if it doesn't come from you,
to be the mirror my weary eyes can rest in;
other beauty they'd be distressed in;
if it's not like you, my lady, it's death indeed,
being merely glass—no true
mirror's without the silvered back they need.
What a wondrous thing to see
for a poor soul who'd despair
of your kindness toward his miserable estate,
if your lovely eyes on me
glowed with charity and care
to beatify me at my age—so late,
and born the fool of fate.
But if grace and fortune over fate prevail,
through you, then, the stars and crabbed nature fail.

235

  A man within a woman—no, I'd say
a god within speaks, clear
to me who stand, all ear,
so charmed that my very self's cajoled away.
I know, when self's astray
from me—my thanks to her—
I stand outside me and, pitying, size me up.
From passion's vain display
her dear face bids me soar

till other beauty seems a poisoned cup.
O lady, conducting up
our souls through tears and fire to days of bliss,
save me from that old me, self's black abyss.

236

If by its heaven-sent power the mind conceives
a true version of face and form, then roughs in clay
a crude model, the workman's hand and heart in play
confer on cold stone a life, and not just by skill.

The same in art: not a brush is raised until
mind sifts, from its cunning cues, the apt and best
—this even with rough designs—rejects the rest
as it culls, deploys, thinks better of, retrieves.

I'm like that model, as crude as you'd come across,
exalted lady, till born again through you,
elate, pristine, as your cleansing auras reach me.

Where I lack, you add; where I'm rough, you file and gloss
in your kindly care for me. What amends are due
for my furores past, as your ways rebuke and teach me?

237

To one of taste both flawless and robust,
sculpture, our firstborn art, gives deepest joy,
showing—face, limbs—a livelier girl or boy
in clay, wax, marble than our eyes detect.

Although sour grudging time, that feeds on wrack,
maims and dismembers, gnawing flesh and bone,
beauty endures—art salvages alone
for heaven's retrieval our fumblings with the dust.

238

On earth, it's no unworthy soul that nurses
hopes of eternal life, all peace and ease,
by accumulating wealth in currencies
heaven coins for us and life on earth disburses.

239

My lady, how comes it about—what all can see
from long experience—that rough mountain stone
carved to a living form, survives its own
creator, who'll end as ashes in an urn?
    Cause lesser than its effect. From which we learn
how nature is less than art, as well I know
whose many a lively statue proves it so,
which time and the tomb exempt, grant amnesty.
    Mine then, the power to give us, you and me,
a long survival in—choose it—stone or color,
faces just like our own, exact and true.
    Though we're dead a thousand years, still men can see
how beautiful you were; I, how much duller,
and yet how far from a fool in loving you.

240

This face, says art, alone
must live on here in stone
as long as the centuries of time endure.
What's heaven to make of her?
I carved the statue, but she's heaven's own art,
not mortal, but divine
to eyes not only mine.
Too briefly she's on earth, who soon must part,
her perfection crippled, as misgivings start
that a rock survives, while dying stops her breath.
Who's to avenge that death?
Nature alone, her children's work in stone
surviving, while time plays havoc with her own.

241

Through many a year and many a vain assay
exploring, the cunning artist from his thought
a living image wrought

—as death drew near—by chipping at mountain stone.
Things grand in a new way
come to one slowly, and they dwindle soon.
So earth has shown
this face and that as various ages vied,
till trial and error brought beauty its divine
zenith in you. Earth's old then; soon to die:
that's why the terror, tied
to beauty as both entwine,
banquets my hungry soul perversely; I
can't answer which, or why,
most pleases or most plagues, with your face in sight:
great nature's doomsday, or my love's delight.

242

    As, working in hard stone to make the face
of someone else, one images his own,
so, like as not, I've shown
her dull and dismal—her effect on me.
The lineaments I trace
intending hers, ape mine in mockery.
True, any stone might be,
so very hard its heart,
hinting at more than mere resemblance there.
Fact is, her cruelty
so crushes me, I start
doing her, but do my own grievance unaware.
If art has any care
to immortalize great beauty, a softer heart
toward me would assure more radiance in my art.

243

    Whenever remembrance of the one I love
is imaged within my heart, that's firm and frail,
death interposes between the two. I quail;
then all the more death hustles my love away.

Outrageous! Yet from this death my soul today
hopes for a joy passing all earthly kind;
invincible Love, armed fully, speaks his mind,
emptying that quiver of barbs he's master of:
    "We die but once. On earth, no second rising.
Then what's in store for one who, once he tumbles
in mortal love, loves on till death? He learns
    Love's ardor frees the soul by magnetizing
it toward love's glowing core your love resembles,
and the soul, like gold new-fired, to God returns."

244

    If sorrow makes one beautiful (it's said),
to weep, bereaved, for a fair human face
means ill is well, means grace
and life redound from having taken a fall;
sweet turns to bitter instead
when frivolous longing overrides the soul;
nor can foul fortune roll
its wheel so the lowly there
provide a triumph as if flung from high.
A kind, devoted role
is mine, alone and bare,
my poorness a lash and rule of life whereby
the pilgrim soul can spy
its own salvation in sport of love or war:
knowing how to lose beats scavenging for more.

245

    "Say the face I'm speaking of now, hers I mean,
had not refused me its affectionate gaze,
then, Love, how brave a blaze
would you have roused to test me through and through,
if, though but dimly seen,
even now her eyes ignite me, wildly too?"

"The least of love's ado
has he who's never scorned,
since satisfaction kills every desire;
once sated, hope withdrew,
so nevermore—be warned—
can it revive love's sweet and painless fire."
    "Not so. I'd never tire
even if she'd grant me her affection's treasure,
yours also, Love. My longing's without measure."

246

    You revel in my torments, only you,
although the right to love is all I'm asking;
relaxed, you watch my anguish, fairly basking.
Far worse than death, all this you put me through.
If I fill up unto
your dudgeon's height my heart with brimming woe
in hope to die thereof,
what kind of loveless love
won't let me die, but kills me blow by blow?
Dying—that's quickly done,
whereas your dragged out cruelty—slow, slow!
Unjustly tortured, one
wants mercy, even more wants justice though.
My soul's steadfast, and so
I serve, bear up, and wish, no matter when
—no, nothing from you—but then
in heaven the martyr's crown, not given by men.

247

    To sleep, even more be made of stone: how these
are sweet, in a world of jobbery and shame.
Not see, not feel or hear: such fortune came
my way. Don't rouse me now. Talk softer, please.

Straight down from heaven, and in the flesh, he came;
then, having seen where fires of justice burned,
and the middling woes of good folk, he returned
to look on God and reveal the eternal light.

Bright star! who made illustrious, in despite
of wrong, the nest where I was born and bred.
His reward? On the foul earth none at all. Instead
look to the Lord for that, His holy name.

Dante I'm speaking of, so little known
his life and work by that unholy brood,
arms wide to all comers—all but men of worth.

That's the man I'd like to be! Were they my own,
his destiny, exile, genius, hardihood,
I'd give up whatever's happiest on earth.

249

"Your beauty an angel's, Lady, you were meant
for many a lover, yes, for hundreds even.
Now all's a-drowse in heaven
if it let one steal from many what's heaven-sent.
Restore, as we lament,
the sunlight of your eyes, that seem to shun
poor wretches born without a gift so great."

"No, never let troubles cloud your pure intent;
the ravisher robbing you of me, that one,
terrified, can't enjoy his heinous state.
Even so with lovers: they're less fortunate
whenever great surfeit curbs their great desire.
Far better wretchedness with live hope afire."

All there's to say of him, no way of saying;
our eyes are blurred, his radiance too strong.
Simpler to cry down those who did him wrong
than for even our best to match his least of merits.

He plunged, for our sake, where the fallen spirits
endure their doom, then off he soared to God.
Heaven flung its great gates open at his nod;
earth slammed her narrow doors, and sent him straying.

Inhospitable homeland, of her fame
a niggling nurse! Here's evidence she thrust
the worst of woes on men of greatest worth.

A thousand proofs, but none more damning. Blame
her for of all expulsions the most unjust.
No man his like or likelier walked the earth.

251

There's pleasure in great favors done, but hidden
within may be some dire offense to grate
against our honor, even our life, its weight
so grievous our very health is reckoned less.

A friend, say, gives us wings to achieve success,
meanwhile rigging our path with hidden wire.
A kibosh there on gratitude! Old desire
longs to be warm as once, but feelings deaden.

That's why, my dear Luigi, keep and heed
unsullied the kindness helped my health to rally.
Don't overcloud it now with fouler weathers.

Anger rides roughshod over love. Indeed,
in friendship, if I read its nature truly,
one torment more than tops a thousand pleasures.

Since I'm too obligated,
though pleasantly, to you,
for a kindness that puts pressure on the soul,
independence is fated
by such favors—like one who
has been robbed—to feel pained and saddened, heart and soul.
Direct sun too often stole
strength from the eye it should accustom to
endure more light, light being its stock in trade.
However, it's not my goal
to cripple in me the gratitude that's due.
Too muchness puts too little in the shade
and turns hostile, I'm afraid,
for love would have true friends (and so they're rare)
in status and esteem be an equal pair.

253

Had I, when young, been leery of the glow
then burning round me, now a fire within,
I'd have doused it, thwarting sin,
even more, have ripped the soul from my frail heart
to abort love's mortal blow.
Our primal fault is where the impeachments start.
Unhappy soul, with no evasive art
at hand those early days,
and now on edge to dart
and die in many a blaze
set long ago! The one no flare could faze
in his green age—what truth time's mirror told!—
now the least spark consumes—decrepit, old.

Though bent with age, to me
—so I'll return and nest
as a weight will where it best
lodges but elsewhere, my lady, 's ill at ease—
heaven reaches out the keys.
Love turns them once, then twice,
opening to holy souls that lady's breast;
my rank iniquities
love bans, then lets me rise,
poor wretch, to where God's rare immortals rest.
Thanks all to her, I'm blest
with favors sweet and strange—so mighty too
that, dying for her, I'm given life anew.

255

Your lovely eyes, now bent
on mine, so near me too
I see me in them—you
must see yourself in mine. Yours then present
an old man's grief, torment;
just as I am, I see me all too well.
In mine, you're the brightest star night skies discover.
Angry heaven must resent
that in sweet eyes my ugliness can dwell,
while in my bleary gaze your splendors hover.
The crueller, harsher part
is what's within: you glide
through mine to a warm heart;
yours bar me from inside.
Why? Honorable pride
stands stalwart against meaner minds below:
love wants noblesse in common, youth aglow.

Suppose a lady has no other graces
but one fine feature, well,
should I not only dwell
on that but love what nature, say, misplaces?
Even while it damps our joy,
each homelier part bases
its appeal on reason, praying
we'll excuse and love good nature's bobble there.
Love, though, when it appraises
endowments that annoy,
incensed, just keeps on saying
reason, in its world, doesn't have a prayer.
Yet heaven insists I care
for homely things and love them: that's to say,
just live with blotches and they fade away.

257

Why only at long last, why next to never
that flush of ardor in me stirs, would waken
to carry me high as heaven, my heart taken
where never it dare adventure on its own?
    Could it be that the languorous hollows we bemoan
between one flurry and the next have stressed
seldom and rare is precious, and the best
what's wanted most, but seen far off forever?
    Those vacuities are the night; your glow's the day;
one turning the heart to ice, and one to fire,
the love, the trust, of incendiary heaven . . .

Although it's amply true your human face
is a vision of heavenly beauty here below,
yet heaven's far distant glow
is a haze for me. But yours I can't forsake.
For my pilgrim soul, no place
on roads so rough and steep old muscles ache.
So here's the way I take
with time: my eye by day, my heart by night
are yours. No interval for heaven at all.
Stars of my birth hour make
your splendor seem so bright
my burning urge can't rise, though heaven call
—unless some other enthrall
by grace or favor till I soar above.
What eye can't see, the heart is loath to love.

259

No question but, when my desire's aflame,
it soars, sometimes, its confidence no lie.
If heaven thought all our passion gone awry,
why did God make the very world we're in?
What worthier cause, I'd ask, to love you, then,
than to glorify that eternal peace above,
source of the heaven-born soul in you I love,
and reason enough true hearts are free of blame?
False hope attends on love that dies with dying
beauty of earth, more ashen, breath by breath;
hope brief as the pale fair face is—briefer even.
Sweet is the hope on a shamefast heart relying,
indifferent to wrinkled skin or the hour of death,
and prime executor of our deed to heaven.

Not true that it's always grim with mortal sin,
this love for a ravishing beauty here on earth,
as long as it melts the hard heart, shows its worth
as a target for divine love's arrowhead.

Love shakes, wakes up the soul, grows wings that sped
its skyward flight. Lets even fond fools aspire.
Is the soul's first step—an impatient one—toward higher
stairs to that heaven the sole Creator's in.

That's where the love I speak of longs to be.
Love for a lady's different. Not much
in that for a wise and virile lover's trouble.

One love seeks heaven; the other, earth's vanity;
the soul's home, one; the other wants taste and touch,
eye fixed on the goods of earth, its gaudy rubble.

261

Love long delayed comes kindly, by fortune's favor,
more than a ready "Yes" does, glib and free.
Mine though, long years gone by, means misery;
joy in old age looks forward to—? Not much.

If heaven felt any pity, the least touch,
we wouldn't burn with glaciers round the heart
as I do for this lady. The tears that start,
leaden with age, fall lonelier than ever.

And now, though the evening road leads stark and stormy,
sun glumly smouldering as it goes below,
air dank and chill . . . dark, dark as the shadows climb—

if love burns best when midway in life's journey,
yet, old and near my doomsday, I'm all aglow:
by the lady's grace, decrepitude's my prime.

If a god, Love, can't you do
whatever you would? Then try
to do for me what I,
if I were Love, would happily do for you.
For the beauty we've in view
great longing's hardly right,
much less possession, with the deathbed near.
Make my desire yours too:
can what crushes give delight?
The cost of grace cut short is doubly dear.
I'd also ask: if fear
of death haunts even losers, tell me this:
what of one dying at the pitch of bliss?

263

A woman's beauty, new
to me, spurs, goads me on;
Tierce, Nones not only gone
but Vespers too, with evening in the air.
My birth stars, at set-to
with death, trade pawn for pawn;
fortune and its fruition never square.
To weight of years, to hair
as white as snow I was reconciled, and yes,
held in my hand the pledge of heaven too,
such as a penitent heart assures of us.
He loses more who's less
afraid at nightfall; through
cold valor of age he thinks himself above
all long-gone smouldering love.
If its least whisper tease his memory though,
even old—unless saved by grace—he can't say no.

As I've carried in my heart this many a year
the image, lady, of your face, let Love,
now death impends above,
with his imprimatur on the soul engrave it,
so that, from prison here,
it can slough with joy the heavy flesh earth gave it.
May such an impress save it
through calm and storm—as by
that holy cross that routs the demonic foe—
till it gain, whence nature stole it, heaven on high,
for a model the tall angels, souls aglow,
learn to reproduce, to show
our earth, by that flesh-bound spirit given breath,
how your lovely face stays with us after death.

265

So it wouldn't need to retrieve the total sum
of beauty given so many here on earth,
heaven combined all, in the birth
of a lady serenely beautiful, veiled in white;
to regain such treasure from
the once lovely would have taxed even heaven's might.
With her last breath, not quite
a moment even, God,
from a world but half aware,
took back her beauty, but left our eyes a blur.
Though she's interred in sod,
not all lies buried there;
we've still her charming poems, sweet and pure.
Cruel kindness! her allure
had heaven expended on homely folk instead,
then wished it back through death, we'd all be dead.

What wonder that—seeing how, beside your fire,
I was thawed to warmer life—now the fire's out,
within me I feel it nag and gnaw, about
to shrivel me into cinders, bit by bit.

Their brilliance once aglow, your features lit
(often to my pain) so gloriously the place
that, with a glance, pleasure suffused my face;
torture and death seemed holiday—lute and lyre.

But since heaven's stolen both that cordial flame
and its splendor that warmed my life, sustained it too,
I'm a smothered coal, that's all: brief feeble flashes.

Unless Love comes with fuel, as once he came,
to stoke up fire in the cooling residue,
there remains no spark alive: soon I'll be ashes.

The Four Last Things

1547–1564

A SONNET OF THE EARLY 1550s sounds like Michelangelo's farewell to life:

So now it's over, my day's long voyage, through
tumultuous ocean, in a hull unsteady . . . (285)

But the long voyage was not over. He had a full ten years to live, years often as tumultuous with anxiety, tribulation and triumph as the more active years before. Even the matter of the tomb, which seemed concluded in 1545, was still haunting him in 1553, when renewed contention about it rekindled his sense of shame at a pledge unkept. Concern for his family in Florence weighed on him; he worried about his niece Francesca, frequently ill, and even more about a proper marriage and honorable career for his nephew Lionardo, whose well-meant but bumbling behavior was a frequent annoyance. There was also pressure on him to return to Florence, where his admirer, Duke Cosimo, was impatiently hopeful that he would return to complete the Medici Chapel and other projects left unfinished there.

His health, now that he was in his eighties, was of concern to his friends. Plagued by the infirmities of age, he had twice been seriously ill in the years before Vittoria Colonna died. The arduous work of frescoing was now too much for him; the Pauline paintings he had finished at the age of seventy-five were his last. Partly as a form of exercise, he kept busy for a while with hammer and chisel. In 1547 he began work on the *Florentine Pietà*, but, as centuries later a deranged fanatic was to take a hammer to his more famous *Pietà* in Rome, so Michelangelo, dissatisfied with his new work, attacked it with even greater fury, leaving it in pieces to be salvaged by a young student, who did what he could to reassemble it. Afterward, Michelangelo worked fitfully at the simpler *Rondanini Pietà*, its wraithlike Christ and Mary growing more and more emaciated as he chipped away at it.

But if painting and sculpture were too taxing, architectural design was not. While still working on the Pauline frescoes (for, in Michelangelo's hectic career, project often overlapped 137 ❧

with project) he began his seventeen years of work redoing the basilica of St. Peter's, preparing the solid base for the great cupola he envisaged, and striving to get enough accomplished so that his successors could never undo his work. Various other architectural projects, all imposing—the Farnese Palace, the Capitoline Hill—also engaged him.

From his earliest days, when an infuriated fellow student had left him marked for life by crushing his nose, his talent and acclaim had aroused envy in rival artists and their sometimes influential backers. Envy hardened into enmity, probably never more dangerous than in his later years, when in addition to other pretexts he could now be charged with the incompetence of old age. Time and again his enemies tried to loosen his control over St. Peter's; fortunately the popes of those years were sturdy backers of his genius and for the most part protected him. Even the *Last Judgment*, with its exuberant nudity, came under attack; powerful voices urged its destruction. Though it was spared, a month before Michelangelo's death it was decided the details that had given offense should be painted over. (Those who did the work were known as the "panty-painters.")

Architecture was not the only outlet for his creativity. In the opinion of many it was his poetry that was vigorous now; it grew stronger than ever as painting and sculpture were failing him.

Anticipations of Vittoria Colonna's death in 1547 and the ensuing grief account for many of the dozen or so sonnets and madrigals written that year. After those last memories of her, there are no more love poems for either man or woman, although 263, written perhaps in the ten months after her death, suggests he was still open to temptation by "a woman's beauty new / to me . . ."—a temptation he could resist only by divine help:

> If its least whisper tease his memory though,
> even old—unless saved by grace—he can't say no.

Romantic novelizers of his life would like to think he might have been stirred by Sofonisba Anguissola, whom Vasari believed the best woman painter of the time. Of a noble family of

Cortona and, judging by her self-portraits, quite attractive, she had come to Rome in 1554 for a two-year stay, during which she did have some talks with Michelangelo about her art and was given a sketch of his to color. But neither in his poems of those years or elsewhere is there any hint that the eighty-year-old artist, busy with the architecture of St. Peter's, his thoughts on death, judgment, heaven, and hell—the four last things— had anything to give her but the kindly advice Sofonisba's father wrote to thank him for. What his own focus was on is suggested by the conclusion of a sonnet written during her years in Rome:

> Teach me disdain of all the mad earth prizes,
> beauties I love and made so much of then,
> for eternal life is now life's sole ambition. (288)

He did reflect nostalgically on love itself and on his own suscep-tibility to it:

> So open and broad that avenue, from start
> to finish, that hundreds—thousands!—can't congest it.
> Every age, rank, sex have come; their coming
> blessed it,
> while leaving me fretful, jealous, full of fear . . . (276)

The twenty-five or so poems, half of them unfinished, that be-long to the last seventeen years of his life have a morose but vigorous prelude in the *terza rima* lines of 267. Before Vittoria died, he had asked himself, foreseeing her death,

> What's left on earth you'd care to see again? (229)

In 267 comes the answer: nothing at all. According to the poem, he lives in squalor and confinement in the house he bought some thirty years earlier in Macel dei Corvi, and which the original contract describes as anything but straitened.

Feeling miserable and abandoned, according to the poem, he details the embarrassing ailments of age. Looking back on his love poems, he sees them as fit only for wrapping fish or cleaning toilets. The art he had lived for, the fame once his, have left him, he says in the street language of his youth, old, poor, and alone, like one who "having swum wide ocean, drowned in snot." His only hope is that of dying soon. Not one prayerful word in the poem about God or eternal bliss.

But soon the poems will show that these are his only concerns, and that his intensity burns as brightly there as it ever did in the poems for Cavalieri or Vittoria Colonna:

> O let me see You everywhere I go!
> If mortal beauty sets the soul afire,
> Your dazzle will show how dim it is; desire
> for You burns high, as once in heaven's own air . . .
>   (274)

Except for two or three occasional pieces, the poems to come "add up to one prolonged colloquy with Christ and/or God the Father" (Cambon, 118).

To confirm how dim earthly beauty is in comparison with the divine, he renounces "the world and all its fables" (288); he is contemptuous even of the art that once mattered so much to him:

> The daft illusion once so cuddled there
> that art was my sovereign lord to idolize,
>   I've come to know—how well!—was a pack of lies . . .
>   (285)

He is still haunted, as long before, by the fear that some grievous sin has left him

> in deadly peril
> to my own soul, here chiseling things divine. (282)

His one hope is that he will be given the grace of forgiveness through Christ's "effusion of blood," invoked in several of the last poems.

De Tolnay (114) believes that it was only after Vittoria's death that Michelangelo "created his most beautiful religious poetry," as in these sonnets of renunciation, hope, and divine love. Clements (293) too thinks that in their "peak of religious passion" they are in some ways "the jewels of the canzionere.

Whereas the quality of Michelangelo's sculpture inevitably de-
clined, as the last Pietàs attest, the quality of the poetry soars."
It had never been more simple, concentrated, direct, more free
of occasional artifice. Whereas twenty years earlier he had been
tormented by his desire for an earthly love,

> my long desired sweet lord,
> in my unworthy but eager arms, forever (72)

now his thoughts are on the infinite fulfillment that so many
unfinished statues and poems had in view.

> Painting and sculpture soothe the soul no more,
> its focus fixed on the love divine, outstretching
> on the cross, to enfold us closer, open arms. (285)

On Saturday, February 12, 1564, Michelangelo worked fitfully
at the *Rondanini Pietà*. He had planned to do so the next day,
until reminded that it was Sunday. On Monday, the opening
of carnival week, he was ill with fever. Friends, including Ca-
valieri, were summoned. Sometime in the next day or two he
burned drawings, sketches, cartoons—and no doubt verses—so
that no one would see his less than perfect drafts. He died that
Friday, February 18, two weeks short of his ninetieth birthday.

I'm packaged in here like the pulp in fruit
compacted by its peel. In lonely gloom,
a genii in a jar. Dumped destitute.

No room for flying high. I'm in a tomb
where mad Arachne and her creepy crew
keep jittering up and down, a spooky loom.

My entryway's a jakes for giants, who
gorge on gut-loosening grapes or suffer flux.
No other comfort station seems to do.

Urine! How well I know it—drippy duct
compelling me awake too early, when
dawn plays at peekaboo, then yonder—yuck!—

dead cats, cesspool and privy slosh, pigpen
guck—gifts for me, flung hit-or-miss?
Can't trudge to a proper dunghill, gentlemen?

Soul gets some help from body though in this:
if guts, unclogged, could ventilate their smell
no bread and cheese would keep it in duress,

while round it now catarrh and mucus jell.
Congestion blocks the postern down in back.
With all that phlegm, top exit's blocked as well.

Gut-sprung and graveled, spavined, out of whack,
done in by drudgery's what I am. I pay
innkeeper Death for fleabag, grub and sack.

My pleasure: gloomy moping. Old and grey,
discomfort's my repose. Who'd choose it so,
God keep him in the dumps day after day.

The bogeyman, that's me, at a twelfth-night show.
The setting's right, a stable. Disrepair's
conspicuous near fine mansions in a row.

No flames of love within my heart, a bare
cold hearthstone deep in ash. Chill drafts prevail.
Clipped are the wings that rode celestial air.

Skull hums like a hornet in a wooden pail;
gunnysack skin totes bones and jute around;
bladder's a pouch of gravel, edged like shale.

My eyes: mauve pigment pestled till it's ground;
teeth: oboe-keys that, when I puff out air,
whistle it through or else begrudge the sound.

My face says, "Boo!" It's scary. Rags I wear
rout—without bow and arrow—flocks of crows
from fresh-sown furrows even when weather's fair.

One ear's all spider fuzz. I've tremolos
in the one an all-night vocal cricket chooses.
Can't sleep for my raucous snuffling, mouth and nose.

Amor, flower-quilted grottos, all the Muses,
for these I scribbled reams—now scraps to tot
up tabs, wrap fish, scrub toilets, or worse uses.

The puppets once I postured, cocky lot,
size up my here and now: I'm like the one
who, having swum wide ocean, drowned in snot.

My cherished art, my season in the sun,
name, fame, acclaim—that cant I made a run for,
left me in servitude, poor, old, alone.

O death, relieve me soon. Or soon I'm done for.

268

Because age steals away
past longings deaf and blind,
I've reconciled my mind
to death, being tired, with few last words to say.
In fear and awe today
for what no eye can see,
as from what charms and terrifies me too,
my soul would wave away your lovely face.
But Love, that won't bend a knee
to truth, thrills me anew
with ardent hope, and seems to say, the place
of love outsoars the earth . . .

Now armed with biting ice, now tongues of fire,
now weight of years and grief, now bitter shame,
I see mirrored: what came
is what's to come. Hope dolorously sings
how every joy's a liar,
as bad, being brief, as what affliction brings.
Good fortune and foul too, going round in rings,
share my ennui; I crave their pardon still;
but seeing that all the huddled hours that fill
our life are quick and curt—that's bliss to me!
Death's the best doctor for time's misery.

270

You give me only what you're glutted with;
you want from me what I nor no man has.

271

I fed on you, and with you, many a year
to nourish, Love, my spirit (not to say
in part my body). Desire—its wondrous way!—
sustained by hope, made much of my small worth.
    Exhausted now, I struggle to leave earth,
winging my thoughts for nobler, more secure
zones up above. No longer they allure,
the vows, the plighted words I weep for here . . .

272

Bring back the day the reins hung slack and free
and love rode roughshod over me, intent;
bring back the angelic face, calm, whose descent
into deep sod left all earth's virtue buried.
    Bring back my laboring steps, so many, wearied
by weight of age, by heavy time oppressed.

Bring back spring tears and fever to my breast
if you'd consume me still, as used to be.
    If what you live on, Love, is still that steady
regimen of our grief, our lovesick sighing,
small joy for you in these old shivered timbers.
    My soul, set for death's outer banks, yet ready
to offset your barbs, keeps kindlier arrows flying.
A log burned through won't catch: I'm all dead embers.

273

    Though always one and the same, the one same who
alone made all there is—length, breadth, and height—
reveals itself diversely to us: bright
to some, to others dim, in rain of grace.
    I'm shown what no one else is; others trace
there different features, radiant more or less
depending on our crippled wits, that guess
through reason's wreckage at God's grand ado.
    In more receptive hearts, that face, that worth
(if one dare put it so) take root and cling,
only in such to play their guiding role

        .   .   .   .

    .   .   .   .

he finds conforming with his deeper soul.

274

    Oh let me see You everywhere I go!
If mortal beauty sets the soul afire,
Your dazzle will show how dim it is; desire
for You burns high, as once in heaven's own air.
    It's You alone, my dearest Lord, my prayer
appeals to against passion's futile anguish;
only You can give me vision to distinguish
what I should think, wish, do, though slack and slow.

You tethered me to time, no road-to-bliss way,
sentenced, though stooped and faint, to endless ranging,
shackled in heavy flesh, remissions few.
    What can I do to escape from living this way?
Your power divine is my one chance of changing.
I've nothing to fall back on, Lord, but You.

275

    Enclosed and hidden in a monstrous stone,
from the high mountains in cascading rock
I tumbled to find me in this chockablock
rubble, against all instincts of my own.
    At the sun's birth, by one that heaven's foreshown . . .

276

    Whatever the eye finds lovely, in a flash
carries its ache and poignance to the heart.
So open and broad that avenue, from start
to finish, that hundreds—thousands!—can't congest it.
    Every age, rank, sex have come; their coming blessed it,
while leaving me fretful, jealous, full of fear:
which of these beautiful faces brings me near
to heaven on earth, before these limbs are ash?
    If mortal beauty alone stirs such desire
it's not the love which accompanied the soul
from heaven to earth; it's lower lust, all earthy.
    But if, despite you, Love, it goes much higher,
its quest is a different god—no more in thrall
to the fear you'll vex a carcass worn, unworthy.

Though you with line and color excel, securing
for art such laurels as great nature wore,
even better, you've gained on her, by making more
beautiful her own beauty for our sake;
    and now, with that studious pen in hand, you take
a nobler role, composing, page by page,
works that prove you and nature share the stage,
though you give others survival more enduring.
    Yet any age that ever challenged nature
in conjuring beauty was humbled at the close:
what earth aspires to, dwindles to a sigh.
    But you rekindle, in every form and feature,
lives lost in time's dull ash, both yours and those,
assuring them life beyond the death they die.

278

If leaves aren't what you're wanting,
don't come around in Maytime.

279

Power of a lovely face impels me where?
Nothing on earth so takes me: pure delight
lofts me among the blessed souls, in flight
body and soul. No other grace so rare!
    Created works to their creator bear
close kinship. Can heavenly justice then indict me
if I love, even burn with love? Fair forms invite me
to revere God's dearest dream embodied there.

280

Confused, with itself at odds, soul fails to find
any rationale except some deadly sin
I can reckon with but vaguely—though within
His ken with its infinite pity for the oppressed.

You I'm addressing, Lord. I try my best,
but unless Your blood avails me, all the more
I falter. So *miserere!* as before
You'd help one born to the law Your love assigned.

281

Time was my fire burned high, yes, even on ice;
but now it's ice itself, that raging flame;
your knot, once indissoluble, Love, came
undone; death rules as master of the revels.

  Love once had time and place; all that bedevils
the exhausted soul—the burden and the blame,
last stumbling days of misery . . .

282

In such servility! and all so boring!
mistaken notions! and in deadly peril
to my own soul, here chiseling things divine.

283

The springtime, fresh and green, can never guess
how, at life's end, my dearest Lord, we change
our taste, desire, love, longing—years' debris.

  The soul means more, the more the world means less;
art and impending death don't go together,
so what are You still expecting, Lord, from me?

284

If, in Your name, some image comes to mind,
with it comes apprehension of my death:
then what are talent, art? Lost in thin air.

  But if I think—with others so inclined—
happily, we're born anew on life's same path,
I'll serve You further, if the knack's still there.

285

So now it's over, my day's long voyage, through
tumultuous ocean, in a hull unsteady;
I've come to the world's last anchorage, and make ready
life's log with its every reckoning, foul and fair.
    The daft illusion once so cuddled there
that art was a sovereign lord to idolize,
I've come to know—how well!—was a pack of lies,
such as, to their grief, men treasure yet as true.
    Fond, foolish, the lovesick longings felt before,
what becomes of them, my double death approaching?
One certain-sure, one muttering harsh alarms.
    Painting and sculpture soothe the soul no more,
its focus fixed on the love divine, outstretching
on the cross, to enfold us closer, open arms.

286

My infinite thoughts, so many gone awry,
at last now, in my long life's closing years,
ought to contract to one alone, that steers
me toward repose forever in the sky.
    But, Lord, what am I to do if to my eye
no more Your ineffable courtesy appears? . . .

287

Day in, day out, from childhood long ago,
You were my one sole help and guide, O Lord.
That's why my soul looks confidently toward
Your doubled comfort in my doubled woe.

288

The world and all its fables long ago
took over my time for contemplating God.
Grace?—I dismissed it with a careless nod,
sinning worse than if I'd had a chance at none.

What made some wise made me a witless one,
blind to the way I'd straggled off awry.
Now hope's gone dead, and many a time I sigh
to be disengaged from the self I touted so.
    Shorten the road that heavenward winds and rises,
though shortened, dearest Lord, by half again
I'll need your steadying gesture's admonition.
    Teach me disdain of all the mad earth prizes,
beauties I love and made so much of then,
for eternal life is now life's sole ambition.

289

There's nothing lower on earth, of less account
than I feel I am, and am, Lord, without You.
What fluttering faint breath I've left must sue
for pardon from You—You, height of my desire.
    Lower that chain, I pray, Lord, its entire
length, link by link, each strung with gifts from heaven;
faith's chain, I mean; I'd cling there and have striven,
mea culpa, in vain; grace fails; I try but can't.
    This gift of gifts is all the more a treasure,
for rare is precious, and rare it is. The earth,
void of it, 's void of peace, void of serenity.
    Giving blood, you didn't stint; gave without measure.
What good's your gift though? Wasted all its worth
unless heaven opens to this other key.

290

Rid of this nagging nattering cadaver,
dear Lord, and tattered all my bonds with earth,
like one worn out, a sprung old skiff, I'd berth
back in your halcyon cove, foul weather done.
    The thorns, the spikes, the wounded palms each one,
your mild and kindly all-forgiving face,
promise me full repentance, thanks to grace
rained on my somber soul—and reprieve forever.

Don't judge with justice as your holy eyes,
and your ear, as pure as dawn, review my past;
don't let your long arm, hovering, fix and harden.
    Let your blood be enough to purge for Paradise
my sump of sin, and, as I age, flow fast
and faster yet with indulgence, total pardon.

291

I think, indeed know well, some crushing sin,
hidden from me, torments my very soul.
Fire of the sensual flesh, out of control,
left a heart at war, left longing without hope.
    But, Love, one close to you—now must he mope
that grace may fail before death takes his toll? . . .

292

How very sweet indeed the prayers I'd say
if you'd allow me grace enough for praying.
My soil's much too impoverished for purveying
any good fruit by effort of its own.
    Of all work pure and true, no one has sown
but You the seeds now burgeoning, row on row.
None on his nerve alone ventures to go
behind You, unless You show the hallowed way.

293

Burdened with years and crapulous with sin,
bad habits ruggedly rooted, no control,
I see impend two deaths, of body, of soul,
but am feeding my heart on poison none the less.
    For myself, no strength I can muster in distress
is enough to change my ways, life, love, or fate,
unless You show the road, Who illuminate
with your *do* or *don't* the muddlement we're in.

Not enough! Not enough, dear Lord, that You
     give the wish
to set my sights heaven-high. Wish won't insure
that my soul, next time from nothing, is made anew.

   Before You undress it quite of its threads of flesh,
cut half from the high steep trek I now endure,
so I'll have heaven's destination full in view.

294

   It leaves me plunged in gloom and pain—yet dear
is every thought bringing remembrance back
of time gone by, though, rueful, I ransack
annals of wasted days I can't amend.

   So sweet, however, to learn, before my end,
how duplicitous every human pleasure;
but sad because, death looming near, full measure
of pardon for such a burden of sin is rare.

   We've trust in all your promises, and yet
I may presume, O Lord, daring to hope
when repentance lags, you'll set the sluggard free.

   Your effusion of blood! with that we can't forget
there's no parallel to your wretched end. The scope
of your love's no less, with its gift: infinity.

295

   Assured of death, of its timing, though, not so;
life's never long; now there's little left at all.
Joy thrills the sense, but this life's a meager stall
for the ample soul, pleading with me to die.

   A blind world, ours, where bad examples vie
with good and soon run them under, even the best.
All light's gone out, all valor's dead, debased
fraudulence struts; truth cringes and lies low.

   When's it to come, O Lord, what all await

who count on You? Disconcerting, the postponement
numbs hope, leaves the weak soul likelier to waver.
     Your pledge to enlighten the world, what good?—if straight
away death comes, transfixing us (no atonement!)
to our last vain thought—in that frozen pose, forever.

296

     If our very thirst for longer life bids fair
to promise my many years yet even more,
that doesn't mean death's not huddling at the door
or, seeing me unconcerned, holds off a while.
     Why want more life for enjoyment's sake? Exile,
grief, desolation—that's where the Lord's adored.
But high on the hog long years—what's underscored
by that but: the merrier, the more mischief there.
     If, thanks to your grace, sometimes, my dearest Lord,
zeal in its fiery impulse storms the heart,
encouraging comfort and trust—doubt in suspension—
     since no resources I dare call mine afford
such élan, that's when my heaven-bound thrust should start.
The longer we lag, the less our good intention.

297

     Though years and years in dour allurement lapped
cry out for equal time to purge the soul,
"No time!" rules imminent death. And no control,
with the wicked will in what it chose entrapped.

298

     With no less joy than grief and consternation
that You, not they, were the victim doomed to die,
the chosen souls saw great gates in the sky
swing wide—Your blood the key—for mortals here.

Their joy: in seeing Your creature in the clear
after primal guilt and its aftermath of loss;
their grief: aghast at Your agony on the cross,
a servant of servants and true love's oblation.

Who You were, come from where, heaven lavished clues:
all its bright eyes went dim, rock bottom split,
the mountains shuddered, and pitch-black the sea.

He raised the elders from their glum venues,
found for lost angels a more dolorous pit.
Only man, at His font reborn, sang jubilee.

299

For the sugar, for the mule, those candles too,
for the magnum of malmsey added on the side,
no way my resources had adequately replied.
With his scales, St. Michael could even up, no doubt.

Much windless weather has brought my boat about,
sails slack and flapping on the languid sea;
a craft too flimsy at best, it looks to be
a lone straw tossing in the frothy slew.

Compared to your magnificent gifts, that came
a welcome addition to my livelihood,
candlelight, wine, the long-eared means of motion,

supposing, dear friend, I gave you all I am,
I couldn't return in kind—and if I could
trading gift for gift falls short of true devotion.

300

By merit of grace, the cross, and all we've suffered,
Monsignor, we'll meet in heaven; that I know.
Before we breathe our last though here below
how pleasant if we could still meet, you and I.

What if rough road's between, the mountains high,
the ocean wide—no matter. The spirit's eager;

no ice could balk us and no snow beleaguer,
no noose could trip us. The wings of thought are tougher.
    On them, I'm with you always in my mind.
Now, though, I weep for my Urbino dead,
who, were he with us yet, might well be where,
    as planned, we'd meet together. But now I find
his death, still beckoning, lures me on ahead
to a place reserved for both. He's waiting there.

301

    My eyes are saddened by so much they see,
my heart by every single thing on earth.
Except that You gave me You Yourself—Your worth,
Your kindness and Your love—what's life to me?
    My wicked ways, the allure of vanity
amid the shadows of the life I live,
O help me counter these, help and forgive!
Make this—now You've shown us You—our guarantee.

302

    One way remains to loose me yet, dear Lord,
from love, that passion treacherous as inane:
make things go wrong; make weird disasters rain
on me as on Your friends; estrange the world.
    You peel of flesh the same souls You appareled
in flesh; Your blood absolves and leaves them clean
of sin, of human urges, all that's mean . . .

The Text of the Poems

I N 1542, WHEN MICHELANGELO was nearly seventy years old, he and two friends began preparing what would have been the first collection of his poems for publication. One hundred five poems were numbered, one assumes with some regard for chronology, and made ready for the press. The project was abruptly dropped four years later when Luigi del Riccio, one of the friends, suddenly died.

Of the three hundred or so poems we now know, only a handful had been printed in Michelangelo's lifetime. Some were known to the few friends he shared them with. Michelangelo seems to have written and rewritten many of his poems again and again, on whatever paper was at hand: sketches for his art and architecture, the backs of letters, his own or another's receipts, expense accounts. Not many can be dated with precision; experts differ by as much as thirty years in trying to place them. Nor is it always certain for whom they were written; three experts may each attribute a poem to a different designee. Sonnets, madrigals, stanzas in *ottava rima* occur in no order; the some three hundred poems have been called "a horrible mixture of forms."

It wasn't until sixty years after his death that a grandnephew, Michelangelo the Younger, published, in 1623, an edition of the poems. A writer himself, he took the liberty of sanitizing the texts; anything that might have reflected discreditably on the family or fame of Michelangelo was made respectable. Love poems addressed to a *signor* were revamped to fit the *madonna* of tradition; dubious political or religious views were amended. If a sonnet was unfinished, Michelangelo the Younger might finish it in his own genteel way. For two and a half centuries these discreetly doctored verses were the only ones known to the reading public; yet, even so, enough of their power came through to win the admiration of such readers as Wordsworth and Emerson.

In 1863 the real Michelangelo began to emerge when Cesare Guasti published his handsome *Le Rime di Michelangelo Buonarroti, Pittore Scultore e Architetto*, "taken from his own manuscripts."

Classifying the poems according to form—Epigrams and Epi-taphs, Madrigals, Unfinished Madrigals, Sonnets, Unfinished Sonnets, etc.—Guasti set a precedent by writing a prose para-phrase for each poem, of which he often gave several versions. Of the seventy complete sonnets he included, he dedicated some "A Vittoria Colonna" or "Alla Medesima" ("To the same"). Cavalieri isn't credited in such dedications as inspirer of any of the poems.

Next came the publication in 1897 of Dr. Karl Frey's solid *Die Dichtungen des Michelagniolo Buonarroti, herausgegeben und mit kritischen Apparate,* a book attractively republished in Berlin in 1965. The poems are neatly printed without comment, fol-lowed by 280 pages of notes on text and poems.

What is regarded as the basic text today is Enzo Noè Gi-rardi's *Michelangiolo Buonarroti, Rime, con Varianti, Apparato, Nota filologica* (Bari: Editori Laterza, 1960). Girardi establishes as logical an order for the poems as the difficulties permit. He has excellent paraphrases of Michelangelo's often difficult meaning in his some four hundred pages of notes, variant readings, etc.

The two editions of the poems used here, those by Ettore Barelli and Paola Mastrocola, are both based on Girardi's edition.

Translating Poetry

POETRY, SAID ROBERT FROST, is what is lost in translation. In one kind of translation, of course it is; in another kind, we may be able to save some or even much of it. There are two heresies in translation theory which, when applied to poetry, condemn it to instant death. The first is the notion that poetry can be translated literally, "word for word." This practice has limited utility as a learning tool, a step toward reading the poem in its original language, to which the reader means to return for what is lost in translation.

But it has been condemned by poets and poet-translators for almost as long as we have known the written word. Cicero was perhaps the first to do so, though better known is Horace's admonition to those translating Greek plays into Latin: it should not be done *verbo verbum*—word for word. St. Jerome, the great translator of the Bible, agreed: in speaking of Plautus and Terence and their translations from the Greek, he wrote: "Do they stick at the literal words? Don't they rather try to preserve the beauty and style of the original? What men like you call accuracy in translation, learned men call pedantry . . . I have always aimed at translating sense, not words." Centuries later the translators of the King James Bible concurred: "Is the kingdom of God become words and syllables? Why should we be in bondage to them?" Speaking for the centuries between then and now, Dryden, who spent much of his busy life translating and thinking about translation, spoke for scores of others when he wrote: "The translator that would write with any force or spirit of an original must never dwell on the words of the author." Today that conviction is as firm as ever. William Arrowsmith wrote: "There are times—far more frequent than most scholars suppose—when the worst possible treachery is the simple-minded faith in 'accuracy' and literal loyalty to the original." Roger Shattuck, author of the recent *Forbidden Knowledge*, agrees: "The translator must leave behind dictionary meanings and formal syntax . . . Free translation is often not an indulgence but a duty." Two of the best-known collections of critical essays on translation are Reuben Brower's *On Translation* and Arrowsmith's and Shattuck's *The Craft and Content of Translation*. Not a single one of the thirty-three essays—all by distinguished poets, translators, and scholars—has any patience with the notion that poetry can be translated literally. "Clumsy," "absurd," "vulgar," "servile," "half-witted" are only some of the terms that apply to it. And yet there are still those lurking in the dark ages of thought who think that word-for-word translations are "faithful"—"a faith," said Dryden, "that proceeds from superstition."

The second lethal heresy is that poetry is essentially "thought," and that if the translator presents us with the paraphrased meaning of the original he has given us a "faithful" version. It would be hard to find poets who would agree. Surely no poet cared more for the *thought* of his work than Lucretius, whose long poem copes with the very nature of the universe as he saw it. Yet he goes out of his way, twice, to explain that *thought* does not make poetry, unless one turns it to "sweet-speaking song, and, so to speak, touches it with the sweet honey of the Muses":

> *volui tibi suaviloquenti*
> *carmine Pierio rationem exponere nostram*
> *et quasi musaeo dulci contingere melle . . .* (I, 945–47)

By the sweet-speaking song and honey of the Muses he meant above all the rhythm and resonance of his verse, with its harmonic interplay of sound through assonance and alliteration—precisely those elements which the literal translator, his mind fixed on *thought,* thinks beneath his notice and is quick to junk, with pious protestations that this total betrayal of the elements of poetry is what makes for a *faithful* translation!

The concern of poetry is not so much thought itself as "the emotional consequences of thought," as T. S. Eliot has said, perhaps having in mind Wordsworth's conviction that poetry is the "spontaneous overflow of powerful feelings." Other poets have felt, with Robert Frost, that "the sound is the gold in the ore." They might even suspect, as Robert Fitzgerald did, that rhythm itself is the soul of poetry. As Randall Jarrell wrote, "poems are written by memory and desire, love and hatred, day-dreams and nightmares—by a being, not a brain."

Not a brain! Of course the brain is there, trying hard not to show, trying hard to lose itself in the passionate actualities of flesh and blood, or to transcend itself in a world of vision. We all know the anecdote about Degas, concerned because the poetry he wrote never quite came off, although, as he said, he was "full of ideas." Mallarmé, to whom he made his complaint, set him straight; "Poetry, my dear Degas, is not made out of ideas; it is made out of *words*." It was Valéry who, reporting this exchange, italicized *words*, which, since Mallarmé contrasts them with ideas, means words as body and not just as mind. Perhaps our most profound investigator of the poetic process, Valéry insisted that "thought is only an accessory of poetry. The chief thing is the *whole*," by which he meant "the sound, the rhythm, the physical proximity of words, their mutual in-fluences," those elements that end up in the junk heap of the literal translator, his mind on thought alone. Valéry further ob-served: "The true poet will nearly always sacrifice to form . . . any thought that cannot be dissolved into the poem because it requires him to use words or phrases foreign to the poetic tone. An immediate alliance of sound and sense, which is the essential characteristic of poetic expression, can be obtained only at the expense of something—that is, thought."

Michelangelo, like most poets throughout the ages, cared about form, not only in the stone he carved or the wall he fres-coed, but in the lines he wrote. If there was a clash between what he wanted to say and what the form demanded, the form won every time. In all of his poems (except the octosyllabic 21) he expressed himself only in lines of seven or eleven unelided syllables. For most of us, human thought does not naturally flow in such tight channels. Even more constrictive: every sev-enth or eleventh syllable had to have the same vowel sound as one, two, or three other end words within the same few lines—again an outrageous imposition on natural thought. But never once, in all three hundred or so poems, does he let thought interfere with these rigid demands of form, to which it always gives way—and, in doing so, the wonder is, expresses itself all the more vigorously.

Sound and sense—but always the sound that *makes* sense. If these are the essence of poetry, how is the translator to translate and be faithful to both? He starts always, in my experience, with the literal meaning in mind. But, unlike the word-for-worder, he doesn't stop there. He asks himself: is this the kind of idiom an English-speaking poet would use for this idea? Does it have the concreteness we have come to expect of racy English? Does it fit easily into a rhythm like Michelangelo's, or its equivalent in our language? Is the last word of the line one that can find appropriate rhymes, so they can delineate, like marks of a chisel, the outline of a sonnet or *terza rima*? The translator may not be able to match this or that use of such features as alliteration or onomatopoeia, but he should be on the lookout for their aptness everywhere, working for an over-all, if not localized, texture of expressive harmonics or dis-sonances. He is, after all, a poet writing a poem. There is no greater infidelity than passing off a bad poem as representing the good one it is supposed to translate.

If in this discussion I seem to be downplaying thought, it is only to balance the overemphasis too often given its role in literary translation, which should never stoop to being literal. For what we take to be the splendor of poetry is often a splen-dor of language, which may be appareling nothing but banality: "What oft was thought," said the wise poet, "but ne'er so well expressed." Exactly. Heartsore Macbeth is hardly original in thinking

> Tomorrow and tomorrow and tomorrow
> Creeps in this petty pace from day to day . . .
> And all our yesterdays have lighted fools
> The way to dusty death . . .

It is the words and their interplay that work wonders here, not Macbeth's platitudes about time and mortality. When he seems to be choosing thoughts, the poet is choosing words—words in their physical body and with all their affinities and auras, not just their literal meaning—but choosing them so deftly they

Though not the essence of poetry, thought must always seem an essential presence. It may not be the flesh and blood of poetry, but—since poetry invites such figures—let's say it is the structure of bone without which flesh and blood is a vascular disaster. All honor to the honest bones! But need we go so far as to judge a beauty contest by the X-rays of its contenders? Is there any merit in paying homage to a skeleton?

Some technical remarks. In his madrigals, Michelangelo uses lines of eleven and seven syllables, arranged in various rhyming patterns that almost always conclude with a rhymed couplet. I have followed, with very few exceptions, his pattern of rhyme. He sometimes uses identical rhyme; I sometimes use the off-rhyme that has been common in English verse at least since Emily Dickinson. In his other poems—the sonnets, *terza rima*, *ottava rima*, sestinas, *canzoni*, quatrains—he uses the basic Italian hendecasyllabic (eleven-syllable line), with its primary accent on the tenth syllable and secondary accents on the fourth or sixth. These accented syllables are placed where accents would fall in our regular iambic pentameter, which is very like the Italian line, especially when, as in lines like Shakespeare's

To be, or not to be, that is the question . . . ,

it adds that final eleventh syllable. Michelangelo's scansion is somewhat rough to an Italian ear attuned to Dante or Petrarch; I use our iambic pentameter for his hendecasyllabics, but with such liberties as meter has taken in English at least since Wyatt, most conspicuously in poets like Donne.

For the octave (the first eight lines) of the sonnets I have devised a rhyme scheme different from his but more adaptable to the rigors of English rhyming. His octave twice requires sets of four words rhyming on the same sound. How much easier it is to rhyme in Italian than in English can be appreciated if we consider the words *love* and *death* (so common in all poetry!) and their Italian counterparts, *amore* and *morte*. The only usable full rhymes for *love* would seem to be *of* and *above*, with *dove* if one doesn't mind raiding the dovecotes of the Muse, and perhaps *shove* or *glove* if the thought can absorb either. A *rimario* for

Dante's *Commedia* shows that he has found twenty-eight perfect rhymes for *amore*. With *death* our poets are at more of an impasse: all they seem to have is *breath*, *saith* (if they dare to be archaic), and *shibboleth*. Dante uses, in just the *Commedia*, fifteen rhyming words with *morte*. Instead of straining the sense, perhaps having to *shove* it or *glove* it, I devised a rhyme scheme I thought would sound enough like his to satisfy: though line 1 finds its match only in line 8, each of the other six lines of the octave rhymes with a line next to it, as in Michelangelo's octave. In the sestet of his sonnets, Michelangelo nine times out of ten has the scheme ABCABC. A very few times he has ABABAB. I follow the first scheme in all but one.

Acknowledgments

SOME of the translations in this edition have been previously published. I wish to thank the editors of the following periodicals for permission to reprint the poems listed:

America: 87, "I wish I'd want what I don't want"; 285, "So now it's over, my day's long voyage"

Chattahoochee Review: 77, "Supposing the passionate fire your eyes enkindle."

Chronicles: A Magazine of American Culture (May 1997): 105, "My gaze saw no mere mortal on the day"; 106, "From heaven it ventured forth, there must return"; 259, "No question but, when my desire's aflame"; 274, "Oh let me see You everywhere I go!"

The New Criterion: 151, "Nothing the best of artists can conceive"; 236, "If by its heaven-sent power the mind conceives"; 239, "My lady, how comes it about—what all can see"; 241, "Through many a year and many a vain assay."

The Formalist: 6, "If any of those old proverbs, lord, make sense"; 43, "My reason, out of sorts with me."

Great River Review: 26, "Uproot a plant—there's no way it can seal"; 27, "Flee from this Love, you lovers"; 36, "My lover stole my heart"; 237, "To one of taste both flawless and robust"; 279, "Power of a lovely face impels me where?" 283, "The springtime, fresh and green."

Harvard Magazine: 5, "A goiter it seems I got from this backward craning."

Light Quarterly: 20, "Sweeter your face than grapes are."

Paris Review: 298, "With no less joy than grief and consternation"; 301, "My eyes are saddened by so much they see"; 302, "One way remains to loose me yet, dear Lord."

Poetry: 152, "As by subtracting, my lady"; 229, "Be sure, my eyes, you know"; 235, "A man within a woman—no, I'd say."

Poetry International: 248, "Straight down from heaven, and in the flesh, he came"; 250, "All there's to say of him, no way of saying."

Sparrow: 148, "I'd feel the more secure"; 149, "I'd surely be thought a dullard in talent, art."

Notes

1. Ca. 1503–4. This is probably the first quatrain of a sonnet and the third and fourth lines of the second quatrain.

2. 1503–4. This is either an independent quatrain or the beginning of a sonnet.

3. Ca. 1504. Sonnet.

4. 1507. Sonnet. Written "in a hasty, youthful scrawl" (Clements, 326) on the back of a letter from Michelangelo to his brother, dated December 24. The poem has been called "For a beautiful Bolognese," and has similarities with Poliziano's unfinished "Stanze per la giostra" (1476–78) (Clements, 204–5), in which there appears a golden-haired nymph wearing a flowery garland, and in which a garland of gold and oriental jewels is described in passages that share with Michelangelo's sonnets some rhyming words. While Michelangelo may have remembered the girl, the garlands, and even the rhymes, most of the poem is his own. Poliziano's poem was first published in 1494 in Bologna, a few months before Michelangelo arrived there for a year-long stay. A painting completed a few years later for the Sistine Chapel shows a woman in a tightly laced bodice and loose skirt, with a knotted cord around her waist. Michelangelo's family had been involved in the textile industry, and he had considered setting up a textile shop for his brother.

5. 1509–10. *Sonetto caudato* [sonnet with tail], the tail consisting of six additional lines at the end of the sonnet, as in 25. It was written while Michelangelo was painting the ceiling of the Sistine Chapel (1508–12). In the margin of the manuscript the artist has drawn an image of a strained figure with a bent back painting a ghostly shape on the ceiling. The "Giovanni" of line 18 refers to Giovanni da Pistoia, a member of the Florentine Academy who sent several sonnets to Michelangelo, whose own letters confirm his extreme discomfort at the time.

6. Ca. 1511. Sonnet. This complaint about ingratitude and mistreatment seems directed against Pope Julius II. The sword (line 10) is a reference to the pope's warlike spirit, and the tree (line 14) refers to the family name, della Rovere ("of the oak"). It is unlikely that the poem was ever actually sent to the pope.

7. Ca. 1511. Madrigal.

8. Ca. 1511. Madrigal, probably unfinished.

9. Ca. 1511. Quatrain, perhaps the beginning of a sonnet. The last line may refer to someone beautiful or to something beautiful in art or nature.

10. 1512. Sonnet. This is a complaint about the corrupt clergy and militaristic policies of Rome under Pope Julius II, the "triple hat" of line 10. It was signed "Your Michelangelo in Turkey," perhaps recalling that Savonarola had called the Roman clergy worse than the Turks (Clements, 129). Michelangelo's sculpture the *Risen Christ*, completed in 1520, has been seen as a visual counterpart to the sonnet: the true Christ as opposed to the image of Christ peddled by those in power.

11. 1513–18. Madrigal. Apparently this text, as well as 12, was transcribed by Michelangelo the Younger from a lost original.

12. 1513–18. A version of this madrigal was set to music by Bartolomeo Tromboncino of Verona and published in 1518 in Naples.

13–14. Ca. 1520. Michelangelo had begun work on the Medici Chapel, for which a few years later he would complete the sculptures *Day* and *Night* for the tomb of Giuliano de' Medici. Both short prose pieces, generally included in editions of his poetry, deal with the sculptures. Although they are simple in appearance, commentators seem to have found them obscure and have interpreted them differently. They are related to the basic idea of the Chapel design: the immortal soul, its values and achievements, survive even when death frees it from the earthly bonds imposed on it by the inexorable onrush of time.

15. Ca. 1520. Generally considered a madrigal, although the rhymes are arranged as the last ten lines of a sonnet.

16. Ca. 1520. Fragment.

17. 1521. Incomplete sonnet. Evidently written in haste on the back of a letter sent to Michelangelo in Carrara. The missing lines obscure the intended conclusion.

18. 1522. The unrhymed last line is evidence that the poem is unfinished. Suggestions of Dantean allegory, as in lines 1 and 5, are rare in Michelangelo. The "fiery sword," with its allusion to Genesis 3:24, may suggest a fall from grace.

19. 1522. Unfinished madrigal.

20. 1518–24. Burlesque verses in *ottava rima*. Among the models for this rural love poem is possibly Lorenzo de' Medici's "La Nencia da Barberino." After mentioning the coral lips of a rural belle it continues:

Inside them are her teeth, a double row,
and whiter than a horse's are, by far.
How many? Left and right some twenty show . . .

In updating Michelangelo's horseplay, here the translator has dealt more freely with his verse than in poems of a more serious nature.

21. 1524 or earlier. This carnival song for men masked as cadavers recalls the *danse macabre* and the gloom of Savonarola's day in Florence. Clements (289) has recalled that it was set to music by Luigi Dallapiccola in "Tre poemi" (1949), and that "dodecaphony heightens the forlorn mood and desperation of the poem."

22. 1524. *Canzone.* Mastrocola summarizes the poem as "an autobiographical meditation [like 33] on the flight of time, lost youth, the approach of death, hostile fortune, the cruelty and imprisonment of love."

23. 1524–25 or 1527–28. Sonnet.

24. 1524–25. Unfinished sonnet.

25. Ca. 1524–25. Like 5, a *sonetto caudato.*

26. 1520s. Two quatrains, perhaps the beginning of a sonnet.

27. 1524–25. Unfinished sonnet. Written on the back of a design for the Medici tombs. Other poets Michelangelo would have known, from Petrarch on, had composed poems advising lovers to flee love. Clements (113) believes that the poem may describe Michelangelo's "unhappy passion" for Gherardo Perini, like other poems from the same period.

28. 1524–26. As the unrhymed last line indicates, this madrigal is un-
finished.

29. 1524–26. Fragment.

30. 1524–26. Madrigal.

31. 1525. Madrigal. The left margin of the manuscript has been cut;
the beginning of each line has been conjectured by Enzo Girardi.

32. 1525. Unfinished sonnet. Clements (224): "the most guilt-ridden
poem."

33. 1524–28. Unfinished *settina*. The manuscript is "almost illegible,"
since Michelangelo has written over it in ink. The poem's restoration, some-
times conjectural, is the work of Enzo Girardi. The proper end words of
lines 11 and 12 have been reversed in Michelangelo's text, as well as in the
translation.

34. Ca. 1526.? Sonnet.

35. Ca. 1526. Unfinished *terza rima*. The poem has been described as
"seemingly an instruction on the painting of the eye" (Clements, 76). How-
ever, its puzzling content has elicited from Italian commentators such re-
marks as *"molto oscuro"* and even *"oscurissimo."*

36. 1524–25. Two quatrains, probably the beginning of a sonnet. The
lover is possibly Gherardo Perini.

37. 1520s. In form, the sestet of a sonnet. The "you" addressed appears
to be love, human or divine.

38–40. 1520s. Unfinished sonnets.

41–42. After 1528. Sonnets.

43. After 1528. Sonnet. The two deaths in line 12 refer to the death
of emotional life if he rejects the temptation of love, and the death of his
immortal soul if he gives in to it. In line 6 the phoenix is the mythical bird
fabled to die every five or six hundred years in a fire started by the sun and
then to rise from its own ashes with renewed youth to live another cycle.

44. After 1528. Unfinished sonnet.

45. Ca. 1528. Unfinished *capitolo, terza rima*. The death of his brother
Buonarroto in 1528 may have moved Michelangelo to begin this poem.

46. After 1528. Sonnet. On the death of a friend who had helped and
inspired Michelangelo, perhaps his brother Buonarroto. The image of the
heavenly hammer in God's workshop is from Dante's *Paradiso*, II, 127–32.

47. After 1528. Sonnet. It is not certain whose death is referred to
here. If the poem was written for Febo di Poggio, as Girardi suggests, the
date would more likely be 1534–35.

48. Ca. 1528. Perhaps a tercet from a sonnet or a fragment of a *terza
rima*.

49. Ca. 1530. Quatrain.

50. Ca. 1530. Fragment, probably the beginning of a sonnet.

51. 1528–30. Unfinished *canzone*. Clements (290) believes that this la-
ment for lost time reflects Michelangelo's depression over the three years he
had wasted on the facade of San Lorenzo (1517–20).

52. 1531. Unfinished sonnet.

53. 1531. In form, the sestet of a sonnet. In line 1, *cavalca* [rides] has

been seen as an off-color reference to Tommaso de' Cavalieri, whom, however, Michelangelo did not meet until 1532, and whom he never addressed indecently. See note 58.

54. 1531-32. *Ottava rima* (stanzas four and five incomplete).

55. 1531-32. Stanza of *ottava rima*, although one authority has referred to it as the "octave of an incomplete sonnet." It is not clear to whom it was addressed.

56. 1532. Quatrain or the beginning of a sonnet.

57. 1532. Probably the beginning of a sonnet.

58. 1532. Sonnet. Probably the first poem to Tommaso de' Cavalieri.

59-61. 1532. Sonnets for Cavalieri.

62. 1532? Sonnet, probably for Cavalieri.

63. Date uncertain. Sonnet. The imagery here is of flint and steel; the fire they start can reduce stone to the powder from which the enduring mortar is made. Some scholars believe that the *gold* (rather than steel) of the last line refers to Cavalieri.

64. Date uncertain. Girardi, Cambon and others believe that this is a complete poem. The original is written out in large, handsome lettering.

65. 1532. Unfinished sonnet. The last line is reminiscent of Michelangelo's drawing of *The Archers*, which de Tolnay believes was among the mythological drawings given to Cavalieri. Others think that the drawing was completed earlier.

66. 1532-33. Sonnet.

67. Shortly before 1534, according to Girardi, on the basis of the handwriting. *Ottava rima.* Other suggested dates range from 1527 to 1556—a spread of thirty years. On "the loveliness and intact simplicity of rustic life versus the menacing corruption of city life, [followed by] what looks like an allegorical sequel [68] on the gigantic power of the vices that breed there" (Cambon, 59). Late in life Michelangelo wrote to Vasari: "I'm sure peace is not to be found anywhere except in the woods."

Wordsworth translated the first four stanzas, beginning with "And sweet it is to see in summer time / The daring goats upon a rocky hill . . ."

68. Ca. 1534. *Ottava rima*, apparently unfinished. An example of Michelangelo's "curious preoccupation with giants" (Clements, 166).

69. Probably ca. 1534. Two tercets that appear to be the conclusion of a sonnet. This poem was written on the same sheets as 67 and 68.

70. Ca. 1534. *Sestina.* Like 33, this work is almost illegible and has been restored by Girardi. The proper end words of lines 28 and 29 were reversed by Michelangelo and in the translation as well. One of the six end words is *lega* [binds], which becomes *bound* in the translation. It refers to the powers of love and fate. Images of binding are frequent in Michelangelo's love poems—one of the contradictions in a nature so independent? As one of his friends had said to him years earlier, he had defied the pope in a way the King of France would not have dared to. As Vasari (366) has said, he had freed the artists of his time and afterwards, "seeing that he broke the bonds and chains that had previously confined them to the creation of traditional forms." The "cruel star" of line 1 introduces the question of astrological determinism or free will; Michelangelo's own horoscope is mentioned both

by Condivi and Vasari, who says that "the child's horoscope ... showed Mercury and Venus in the house of Jupiter, peaceably disposed: in other words, his mind and hands were destined to fashion sublime and magnificent works of art" (Vasari, 326).

71. Ca. 1532–34. *Sonetto caudato.* Commentators disagree about whether the poet is genuinely angry or is having fun at the expense of a Pistoian friend, quite possibly Giovanni da Pistoia, (see note 5), who had sent him some sonnets. Dante, the "great Poet" of line 12, despised Pistoia (see *Inferno*, XXV, 10–12).

72. Ca. 1533. Sonnet. For Cavalieri. Lines 10–11: it was thought that time and its astronomical manifestations would end on Judgment Day.

73. 1533. For Cavalieri, probably the beginning of a sonnet. The speaker is the feminine *anima* [the soul].

74. 1533. Octave of a sonnet. Probably for Cavalieri.

75. Ca. 1533. Unfinished sonnet, apparently. This unusually playful poem was probably for Cavalieri.

76. Summer, 1533. Sonnet. Probably for Cavalieri, although among the earlier drafts *donna* (lady) appears in line 12, instead of *signor* (lord).

77–78. 1533. Sonnets. Probably for Cavalieri.

79. Ca. 1533. Sonnet. For Cavalieri, to whom Michelangelo had given, or was about to give, some mythological drawings with erotic overtones. The friend of line 9 is someone who served as an intermediary between them. In line 10 "gracious ... grateful ... grace ..." represent Michelangelo's *"grazia ... grazia ... ringrazia ..."*

80. Ca. 1533. Sonnet. Probably for Cavalieri.

81. Between 1526 and 1546 Michelangelo wrote some twelve versions of this madrigal. Earlier versions are addressed to a lady; the later ones seem intended for Cavalieri.

82. Ca. 1534. Sonnet. For Cavalieri.

83. Ca. 1534. Sonnet. For Cavalieri. Lines 5 and 6 refer to gossipy insinuations that there was something immoral in Michelangelo's love. It is "among the most explicit and important" of the poems (Barelli).

84. 1534. Sonnet. Probably for Cavalieri. See 151 for this theory of artistic creation: the finished work is potentially embedded within the material, whether it is stone or pen and ink.

85. 1533–34. *Capitolo, terza rima.* Allusions and in-jokes make the poem difficult for readers today. Francesco Berni, a writer of burlesque poetry, had sent a letter in verse praising Michelangelo to Sebastiano del Piombo, a painter and friend of Michelangelo, whose poem pretends to be an answer from Sebastiano, who had recently become a friar ("Brother"). Michelangelo puns on the name "Medici," (*medico* means "doctor"): the "Medicee-man" is Giulio de' Medici, then Pope Clement VII; the "Medicee the Less" is Cardinal Hippolito de' Medici, whose secretary, "good at hush-hush," was Francesco Maria Molza. The "hangman" was Michelangelo himself; Raphael had called him that to deride his apparent sobriety. "Meathead" puns on the name of Monsignor Carnesecchi ("dried meat"). Some of Michelangelo's more down-to-earth poetry was influenced by the coarsely humorous burlesques of Berni, who in his letter praised Michelangelo in compari-

son with other poets of the time, because "He says things; you say words."

86. Early 1530s. *Capitolo, terza rima,* unfinished. The date of Michelangelo's father's death is uncertain. Some authorities place it in 1531, others in 1534. Recently there seems to be more evidence for the early date.

87. Ca. 1534. Sonnet. Although Girardi believes that the handwriting and paper date this to "the Cavalieri period," the reference in line 13 to the "comely bride," often used in connection with the soul or the church by religious writers, suggests that it may belong among the later religious poems (1550–54). Bull believes that the plea of line 9 anticipates the violent conversion of St. Paul, depicted in the Pauline fresco of 1542–45.

88–89. 1532–34. Sonnets. For Cavalieri.

90. 1532–34. Sonnets. Probably for Cavalieri. Cf. Mark 8:23 and John 9:6 for accounts of Christ giving sight to the blind with his spittle.

91. 1534–36; reworked in 1546. Madrigal. Probably for Cavalieri. Commentators have referred to this madrigal as "somewhat labored" and even "tortuous." According to one it is "at Michelangelo's mannerist worst" (Cambon, 62).

92. 1534–36. Madrigal. Probably for Cavalieri.

93. 1534–36. Madrigal. For Cavalieri. The senses, heart, soul and reason parallel the scheme of the four bodily humors. Some take "the one" (line 10) to be one of the sighs; others, one of the pair *senses/heart.* This madrigal was set to music by the Flemish composer Jakob Arcadelt (ca. 1504 to after 1567), a choirmaster at St. Peter's in Rome.

94. 1535. Sonnet. Probably for Cavalieri. The "poor thing" is the silkworm. At about the time this was written Michelangelo was thinking about or working on the *Last Judgment* in the Sistine Chapel, in which he painted St. Bartholomew, who was martyred by flaying, holding his own skin, the deformed face generally believed to be Michelangelo's self-portrait.

95. 1534–38. Sonnet. Probably for Cavalieri. Imagery from nature is as rare in Michelangelo's poetry as in his painting.

96. Ca. 1534–38. *Capitolo, terza rima,* unfinished. Apparently for Cavalieri.

97. Shortly after 1534. Sonnet. For Cavalieri. Other suggestions for the reference of "His" (here capitalized) of line 14: Cavalieri, art itself.

98. Date uncertain. Sonnet. Written for Cavalieri, as the pun in the last line makes clear, and as Varchi also testified in his 1547 lecture. But it is also possible that it belongs with the earlier poems for Cavalieri. Saslow has suggested that it was done around the time Michelangelo did his drawing of the punishment of Tityus, among those given to Cavalieri within a year or so of their meeting. The drawing represents Tityus, who was guilty of rape, bound to a rock, while his continually regenerating liver (the seat of lust) is continually devoured by a vulture.

99. 1535? Sonnet. Apparently inspired by the death of the young Florentine Febo di Poggio ("Phoebus of the Hill") or by a break in his friendship with Michelangelo, perhaps on the older man's move to Rome late in 1534. The biblical reference in line 10 is to Psalm 119:105, "Thy word is a lamp unto my feet . . ."

100. 1535? Allusions in this unfinished and cryptic sonnet are clarified by the name of the young man to whom the poem is addressed: Febo di Poggio, *Febo* is Phoebus, the sun god; *Poggio* means "hill," as referred to in line 8. Interpreters differ on whether the "bird" of line 5 is the eagle, thought to have the power of gazing open-eyed at the sun, or the phoenix, reborn after its fiery (solar) death.

101. 1535–41. Sonnet. As Mastrocola suggests, the four sonnets on night (101–4) seem like showpieces, with their contradictory mix of praise and disparise and their elaborate artistry. But the night, and time in general, are heartfelt themes for Michelangelo. The tombs of the Medici Chapel, on which he had worked throughout the previous decade, are a grand allegory of the work of time. The sculpture *Night*, the only one to which he gives a voice (247) and her own emblems, moon, owl, etc., is particularly evocative. The cosmic epic of the Sistine ceiling begins with the themes of day and night: the separation of light and dark and the creation of the sun and moon. The four sonnets, Mastrocola believes, are a meditation on the secrets of the universe: the creation of time, the distinction between night and day, which symbolizes what is dark and light in the human being and his destiny. Saslow has recalled that Michelangelo, who slept poorly, often worked at night, having devised a headpiece that held a candle.

102. 1535–41. Sonnet. This is one of Michelangelo's best-known poems.

103. 1535–41. Sonnet.

104. 1535–41. Sonnet. The "you" of lines 12–14 probably refers to Cavalieri. One painting in the Sistine Chapel shows God creating the sun with his right hand, and the moon, behind Him, with his left.

105. 1535–41. Sonnet. Probably for Cavalieri.

106. 1536–42. Sonnet. Many versions. Revised in 1546. For Cavalieri.

107. 1534–42. Madrigal. Probably for Cavalieri.

108. 1534–42. Stanza of *ottava rima*. Perhaps for Cavalieri. For remarks on the phoenix, see note 43.

109. 1536–44. Madrigal. Apparently for Cavalieri.

110. After 1534. It is said that on a wall halfway up a stairway in his home in Rome, Michelangelo drew a skeleton; on its shoulder was a coffin on which these lines were written.

111. 1536. Madrigal. Apparently among the first poems for Vittoria Colonna, whom Michelangelo met that year.

112. The chronology of poems from here to 176 cannot be definitely established. Their composition falls between 1536 and 1542–46, when fair copies were prepared for intended publication. For the most part they remain in the order in which Michelangelo left them. Madrigal. This appears to be the first poem written to "the lady beautiful and cruel."

113. Ca. 1536–38. Madrigal. Probably for Vittoria Colonna.

114. Ca. 1536–46. Madrigal. For the lady beautiful and cruel? For Vittoria Colonna?

115. 1536–42. Unfinished. For Vittoria Colonna or an unknown lady. The poem begins with a jingle of words: *"Lezi, vezzi, carezze . . ."* The unrhymed last line suggests that the poem is unfinished.

116. Ca. 1536–38. Madrigal. Almost surely for Vittoria Colonna.

117. Ca. 1535–42. Madrigal. Probably for Vittoria Colonna. The rhyme in line 9 represents the *l'amo e bramo e chiamo* of the Italian. In line 15, the "her here. Who . . ." is for the Italian *qual qua questa*, considered by Barelli to be "excessive alliteration."

118. 1536–42. Madrigal. Probably for the lady beautiful and cruel.

119. Early 1540s? Madrigal. Probably for the lady beautiful and cruel.

120. 1536–40. Madrigal. This is believed to be one of the first written for Vittoria Colonna. Cambon (157) believes that the strained syntax (the long interruption of lines 6–10) is like Michelangelo's *figura serpentinata* in art—as illustrated by the almost spiraling figure of Mary next to Christ in the *Last Judgment.*

121. Late 1530s. Madrigal. Perhaps for Vittoria Colonna.

122. Ca. 1536–46. Madrigal. Apparently for Vittoria Colonna. Line 5: the salamander of mythology was a lizard-like creature thought capable of existing in fire.

123. 1536–46. Madrigal. For the lady beautiful and cruel. Mastrocola finds in this poem an example of Michelangelo's sometimes complicated reasoning. It opens with a statement followed by "so . . . if . . . if then . . . yet, if . . . then . . . since . . ." and the process leads to a last line that undercuts the first.

124–29. 1536–46. Madrigals. For the lady beautiful and cruel. In 125, however, the word *pietosa* (kind, compassionate) in line 2 suggests otherwise for that poem. In regard to 127, Michelangelo is quoted as saying to his friend Donato Giannotti, as reported in the *Dialogi,* that "a marvelous thing is the effect of this thought of death, which by its very nature destroys all things—preserves and maintains those who think on it, and defends them from all human passions." Michelangelo then recalled that he had pointed this out in a *madrigaletto* about the conflict between love and the fear of death and quoted the poem. As Clements, who quotes these remarks (299), has stated, "if we give credence to these sentiments, they explain why Michelangelo was content to devote so much time to the planning and execution of sepulchers and mortuary chapels." In line 1 of 129 a "star more bright" refers to the sun.

130. 1534–42. Madrigal. Perhaps for Cavalieri. Michelangelo sent this madrigal and 131 to his friend del Riccio with the following note: "You have the spirit of poetry, so please cut and fix up whichever of these two madrigals seems the least bad, because I have to pass them on to a friend of ours."

131. Ca. 1536–42. Madrigal. For Cavalieri?

132. Ca. 1536–42. Madrigal. For Cavalieri? Vittoria Colonna? The lady beautiful and cruel? Or a poem of personal confession? Michelangelo appended a note to the manuscript: "To Messer Donato, fixer-up of things done badly."

133–35. 1536–46? Madrigals. A dialogue between Michelangelo and souls in heaven is represented in 134. In 133, line 13: birthclout, "clout": a piece of cloth, especially a baby's diaper.

136. 1542–46. Madrigal. Michelangelo's appended note to del Riccio

gives a variation on the last two lines, suggesting that he and Giannotti help
in choosing the "least bad" version.

137. 1542–46. Madrigal.

138–39. 1536–46. Madrigals. For the lady beautiful and cruel.

140. 1536–46. Madrigal. For the lady beautiful and cruel. The *Last Judgment*, as Condivi has noted, shows some souls reassuming their bodies.

141. 1536–46. Madrigal. For the lady beautiful and cruel.

142. 1536–46. Madrigal. For the lady beautiful and cruel (although Vittoria Colonna has been suggested).

143. 1536–44. Madrigal. For the lady beautiful and cruel. Sent to del Riccio with a note saying, "Thanks for the melons and wine, which I pay for with this scribble."

144. 1536–46. Madrigal. For the lady beautiful and cruel.

145. 1536–44. Madrigal. For the lady beautiful and cruel. The note on Michelangelo's manuscript reads "This is for the raviggiuolo [a type of soft cheese], the next will be for the olives, if worth it."

146. 1536–46. Madrigal. For the lady beautiful and cruel.

147. 1536–43. Madrigal. For the lady beautiful and cruel. The question and love's answer were once considered separate poems and were set to music separately by Jakob Arcadelt in 1542.

148. Ca. 1536–38. Madrigal. For Vittoria Colonna. On the manuscript a postscript to del Riccio reads: "No use giving a palace to someone who wants half a loaf of bread."

149. 1536–46. Madrigal. For Vittoria Colonna.

150. 1536–40. Sonnet. For Vittoria Colonna.

151. 1538–44. For Vittoria Colonna. According to Clements (5), this is his "most famous sonnet . . . Michelangelo succeeded in reducing his entire theory of art into four lines [1–4]" (14). Varchi also stressed its importance in his first talk to the Florentine Academy in 1547. As Mastrocola has stated, there have been *numerosissimi* explications of the sonnet and its possible sources (Aristotelian and Neoplatonic), but Michelangelo's direct and simple language is clear enough for most of us.

152. Ca. 1538–44. Madrigal. For Vittoria Colonna. Cambon points out that in line 1 the word *levare* (translated there as "subtracting," but more literally meaning "to take away," "take out") is the base of the word *levatrice* (midwife), so that there and in line 10, where it is translated "deliver," it has a maieutic function.

153. 1538–44. Madrigal. For Vittoria Colonna. Of the references to sculpture in his poems, this is the only time Michelangelo has used imagery of metal casting, which he disliked. Cambon (84) thinks that the imagery is poorly handled.

154. 1536–40. Madrigal. For Vittoria Colonna.

155. Date uncertain. Madrigal. It is not clear which "lady" is addressed here.

156. Ca. 1538–42. Madrigal. For Vittoria Colonna. Below Michelangelo's copy of the poem is his note, which reads: "To be worked over by day."

157. Ca. 1542–46. Madrigal. It is not clear which "lady" is addressed. Michelangelo's note to del Riccio here reads: "This is for the trout; the sonnet I mentioned [possibly 159] will be for the pepper, worth less; but I can't write."

158. Before 1542. Madrigal. For the lady beautiful and cruel? For Vittoria Colonna?

159. Ca. 1538–41. Sonnet. For Vittoria Colonna. In a letter Michelangelo sent with the poem, he wrote that he would like to give her something he had made to thank her for her own gifts, but that he is unable to thank her sufficiently.

160. Ca. 1538–41. Sonnet. For Vittoria Colonna. The obscurity of lines 5–8, often noted by commentators, casts a shadow over the sestet. It apparently means that if his gratitude were adequate thanks for the favor he received—the restoration of his soul to spiritual integrity—then he and his benefactor would be on even terms. However, wanting to believe that she is far above him, he prefers to feel ingratitude, since that would leave her still on a higher plane.

161. 1538–41. Madrigal. For Vittoria Colonna. Michelangelo's manuscript has the beginning of a letter to her, in which he mentions a drawing of the crucifixion he had sent her and that he is working on the *Last Judgment*. Ramsden dates the letter to spring, 1539.

162. 1538–41. Madrigal. For Vittoria Colonna. The question at the end is, Which has a lower place in heaven, humble sin or *superchio bene*, which most commentators have taken to mean something like "perfect good." That is the interpretation translated. But *superchio*, the word Michelangelo uses to modify "good," generally suggests excess; to give it that meaning makes Michelangelo's question a different one, which might be translated as "tell me who's lower in heaven (if one could) / the kneeling sinner or the ultra-good?"

163. 1538–41. Madrigal. For Vittoria Colonna.

164. 1541–44. Madrigal. For Vittoria Colonna. While this poem is generally considered a madrigal, it consists of two *sestine*, with a rhyme scheme like the last six lines of a sonnet.

165. 1541–44. Madrigal. For Vittoria Colonna.

166. 1541–44. Sonnet. For Vittoria Colonna.

167. 1541–44. Madrigal. Michelangelo's note on the manuscript reads: "For last night's duck."

168. 1542–46. Madrigal. For the lady beautiful and cruel. Two other texts exist, one of which Cambon (161–63) believes has "equal claims on finality" as an alternative exploration of one of two irreconcilable views, so that they are exercises on a theme (Mastrocola, 212). Although the first seven lines of both versions are the same, the poems develop opposite conclusions. The alternative one could be translated:

If never once, though, she
is moved by pity at my heavy woe
and from heaven there's greater kindness than from her,
what I wish ardently
is that love's earthy glow

be cooled or killed as new reflections stir;
and should it yet recur,
her cruelty toward me, then heaven's my goal,
and not by halfs but wholly, heart and soul.

169. 1542–46. Madrigal. For the lady beautiful and cruel. Michel-
angelo's note to del Riccio reads: "This really is a scribble [un polizino]."

170. 1542–46. Madrigal. For the lady beautiful and cruel.

171. 1542–46. Madrigal. Possibly written for Cecchino Bracci, who
died in 1544. (See note 179.) A note to del Riccio included with the poem
asks him to return "the last madrigal" [possibly 169 or 170], which del
Riccio did not understand, so that he could rework it. His servant had taken
it away so hastily, he said, that there had not been time to look it over.

172. 1542–46. Madrigal. For the lady beautiful and cruel. Clements
believes that the woman is most probably "an allegorical figure representing
the fine arts" (161, 205 and passim). Cambon and others disagree; they con-
sider the poem more realistic, with the figures as artist and model, or per-
haps lady and visitor. Michelangelo's note with the manuscript reads: "I'm
not putting this down as a scribble, but as a dream."

173. Ca. 1542–46. Madrigal. For the lady beautiful and cruel? On the
bluish-gray paper of the manuscript, Michelangelo wrote: "One talks of
divine things in a blue field." This leads Bull to conclude that the madrigal
must have been for Vittoria Colonna (322).

174–75. 1542–46. Madrigals. For the lady beautiful and cruel.

176. 1543? Madrigal. For the lady beautiful and cruel (Barelli), for
Cavalieri (Saslow), or for Vittoria Colonna.

177. 1543. Quatrain, epitaph. When Faustina Mancini Attavanti
("Mancina") died in 1543, her admirer, the poet Gandolfo Porrino of Mo-
dena, sent Michelangelo five sonnets, three praising his *Last Judgment* and
two asking him to do her portrait. Michelangelo responded with this poem
and 178. *Mancina*, her nickname, means left-handed. Many commentators
have found the pun in poor taste.

178. 1543. Sonnet. See note to 177.

179–228. In January 1544, Cecchino Bracci, the fifteen-year-old
nephew of Michelangelo's friend Luigi del Riccio, died. The grief-stricken
del Riccio asked Michelangelo to do a bust or portrait for the tomb. Instead,
Michelangelo—who resisted doing portraiture—wrote in the course of the
year a madrigal, a sonnet and forty-eight quatrains in the boy's memory, en-
couraged and obligated by del Riccio's gifts of gourmet food and wine. Mi-
chelangelo thanked him several times for such gifts as trout, truffles, a
turtledove and a fig bread with accompanying notes. Notes were also in-
cluded to explain the poems or to apologize for how *goffo* (clumsy) he
thought the poems were. In about half of the poems, the dead child is imag-
ined speaking: sometimes the tomb itself is given a voice; other poems are
general reflections on mortality. For Michelangelo's relations with del Riccio
and his nephew, see note 197.

184. *Bracci* is the plural of *braccio* (arm).

186. Michelangelo's note to del Riccio reads: "Our [young] friend
speaks . . ." and then goes on to paraphrase the poem, which is based on the

notion that a general allotment of beauty is available in the universe, and that if someone is lavishly endowed with it, others are deprived.

190. With this poem, Michelangelo's note to del Riccio reads: "When you don't want any more of these, stop sending me things," referring to the gifts of food del Riccio kept sending him. Mastrocola (24) sees in this poem what she calls *uso letterale del figurato* (literalization of the figurative). Figuratively, "a thousand souls" were in Cecchino's heart. But then the figure is taken literally; when Cecchino died, it was 1000 souls minus one, so he was still 999/1000 alive.

192. 1544. The only madrigal among the quatrains for Cecchino Bracci. Michelangelo's Latin, *sine peccata* (without sin), in line 7 is incorrect; *sine* should be followed by *peccato* (singular) or *peccatis* (plural). Did Michelangelo think the rhyme scheme more important than syntax? His note to del Riccio reads: "Not to use Latin *[grammatica]*, even incorrectly, would embarrass me, especially in dealing so often with you." It seems that Michelangelo, like Shakespeare, had "small Latin"—and no Greek.

193. 1544. Sonnet. For Cecchino Bracci. Michelangelo sent a note to del Riccio asking him to change the wording of lines 5–8 to those translated here: "The last four lines of the octave . . . which I sent to you yesterday, are contradictory. So please send it back or put these in place of those, so it won't be so clumsy. Or you fix it up."

194. Michelangelo's note to del Riccio reads: "I didn't want to send it, because it's pretty clumsy. But the trout and the truffles would have put pressure on heaven itself."

195. Michelangelo's note reads: "One who sees Cecchino dead speaks to him and Cecchino replies."

196. Michelangelo's note reads: "Now I've kept my promise to do the fifteen scribbles. I don't owe you any more, unless others come down from heaven, where he is." However, Michelangelo continued to write until all forty-eight "scribbles" were completed.

197. In a much discussed note sent with the poem Michelangelo suggested a variant reading for the third and fourth line, with the perhaps bantering caution that it is a *cosa morale* (moral matter). The original lines, which have been kept, read:

> *fan fede a quel ch'i' fu' grazia e diletto*
> *in che carcer quaggiù l'anima vive.*

This might be translated as

> bear witness for him to whom I was grace and delight
> in what a prison the soul lives down here.

In line 3, the alternative version changes *diletto* (delight) to *nel letto* (in bed); in line 4 it changes the first four words about the prison to *che abbracciava e 'n che . . .* (who embraced (me) and in whom . . .). The alternative reading gives what Cambon (18) calls a "sexually risqué variant." Critics differ as to what it means: Barelli calls it "an unmistakable affirmation of the nature of his relations with the boy." Clements refers to a letter Michelangelo had written to del Riccio three years earlier which seems to describe a "Freudian dream" in which "our idol" (Cecchino), laughingly threatened Michelangelo. The latter asks del Riccio to find out from the boy whether he meant the laughter or the threat. Clements (146) has interpreted this to mean "the boy mocked his senile love." In an age when homosexual activity was "still a mortal sin and a legal crime" (144), early editors tended to ignore these quatrains.

198. Michelangelo's note reads: "For the salted mushrooms, since you don't want anything else."

199. Michelangelo's note reads: "This clumsy thing, said a thousand times, [in thanks] for the fennel."

201. Michelangelo's note reads: "This is the trout talking, not I. If you don't like these lines, don't marinate them any more without pepper."

202. It is not known whether or not such a portrait existed.

206. When del Riccio sent Michelangelo some melons and requested a drawing for the bust of Cecchino, Michelangelo replied: "I'm paying you back for the melons with this scribble. No drawing yet; but I will do it since I'm better at drawing. . . ."

207. Michelangelo's note reads: "For the turtledove . . ."

208. Michelangelo's note reads: "Fix it up your way."

211. Michelangelo's note reads: "Clumsy stuff. The fountain's dry. Have to wait for rain, and you're pushing things."

214. Michelangelo's note reads: "The tomb speaks to whoever reads these verses. Clumsy things; but if you want me to do a thousand there are sure to be all kinds."

216. Michelangelo's note reads: "Above the tomb" (which speaks here).

219. Michelangelo's note here explains that the text should be put "Underneath the head, so it can say this."

220–23. All four were sent to del Riccio on the same sheet. At the end Michelangelo wrote that "since poetry is in the doldrums tonight" he is sending four plain buns for the "costive tightwad's" three honey cakes. "Tightwad" may be a joking reference to someone who contributed fewer memorial verses or other tributes for Cecchino.

228. Michelangelo's note reads: "Just for fun; not because I still owe one."

229. 1544–46. Madrigal. This is one of the last poems for Vittoria Colonna, who, having been ill since 1544, died in 1547.

230. 1544. Sonnet. For the lady beautiful and cruel. A version of a year or two earlier was addressed to a man. The change may have been made with publication in view.

231–32. 1544–45. Madrigals. For the lady beautiful and cruel.

233. 1544–45. Sonnet. Probably for the lady beautiful and cruel. In 1545 Michelangelo was seventy years old.

234. 1545? Madrigal. Probably for Vittoria Colonna.

235. 1545–50. Madrigal. For Vittoria Colonna. In a letter of August 1, 1550, Michelangelo wrote to a friend: "I am sending you one or two of the verses [235 and 236] I used to write for the Marchesa of Pescara, who was devoted to me and I no less to her. Death deprived me of a great friend [un grande amico]." Mastrocola suggests that the use of masculine forms (uomo, amico) shows that Michelangelo saw her as a being less sexually determined in the flesh and therefore closer to God.

236. 1545–50. Sonnet. For Vittoria Colonna.

237. 1545–50. Probably the octave of a sonnet. Perhaps for Vittoria Colonna.

238. Ca. 1545. Quatrain. The heaven-coined wealth is spiritual wealth, virtue. "Disburses" has been taken to mean either expends in good works or squanders.

239. 1538–46. Sonnet. Several versions exist. For Vittoria Colonna.

240. 1544–45? Madrigal. Perhaps for Vittoria Colonna.

241. Ca. 1542–44. Madrigal. For Vittoria Colonna. Michelangelo's manuscript note to del Riccio reads: "Since you want some scribbles I can send you only what I have. Too bad . . ."

242. Ca. 1540–44. Madrigal. Probably for the lady beautiful and cruel.

243. Ca. 1545. Sonnet.

244. Ca. 1545. Madrigal.

245. 1545–47. Madrigal. Michelangelo's manuscript note indicates that lines 7–12 are Love's reply to the poet.

246. 1546. Madrigal. Earlier versions, in *capitolo* form, first to a woman, later to a man, go back over twenty years. This final text, prepared for publication, is to a woman, as indicated by the feminine *te sola* in line 1).

247. 1545 or 1546. Quatrain. Some twenty years after Michelangelo carved the figure of *Night* for the Medici tombs in Florence, he wrote his famous reply to a quatrain by Giovanni di Carlo Strozzi which had praised the statue as follows:

> The Night you see in graceful sleep, we knew
> was carved in marble by an Angel here.
> In sleep—that means she's living. You appear
> doubtful? Then wake her up. She'll talk to you.

The "world of jobbery and shame" expressed Michelangelo's opposition to the authoritarian rule of Cosimo de' Medici. Montale (18) praises it as "a quatrain which gives the loftiest idea of Michelangelo's sublimity, and which has been translated into all the languages of the world." It is the only poem in which the voice of one of his works of art is the speaker (unless we count the prose of 13 and 14).

248. 1545–46. Sonnet. In praise of Dante and dispraise of Florence.

249. 1545–46. Madrigal. This is a rare political poem by Michelangelo. The allegorical dialogue between a lover and his lady, victimized by a ravisher, represents a talk between Florentine exiles and their city when it had come under the absolute power of Cosimo de' Medici. Del Riccio's note on the manuscript tells us that the lady is meant to symbolize Florence.

250. Late 1545 or early 1546. Sonnet. Dante, unnamed, is the subject. Florence is again censured, as in 248.

251. Summer 1544 or early 1546. Sonnet. For del Riccio. The favors probably refer to del Riccio's taking Michelangelo into his home when Michelangelo was ill. The offense probably refers to del Riccio's having something printed that the poet found objectionable. The last line is a quotation from Petrarch, CCXXXI, 4.

252. 1545–46. Madrigal. For del Riccio, who responded with a matching madrigal.

253. 1546? Madrigal. On the manuscript Michelangelo wrote two hendecasyllabic lines, which translate as "Song born at night in the middle of my bed, / to be worked over more tomorrow evening." The lines play on the last lines of Petrarch's *sestina* (CCXXXVII): "Song born at night in the middle of the woods, / you'll see a prospering shore tomorrow evening." Michelangelo's second postscript reads: "It would be sweet as the apples of Adam, but in my body I have no apples." A possible pun: *mele* means "apples"; *miele* means "honey."

254. 1546? Madrigal. Perhaps for Vittoria Colonna? Michelangelo's postscript for del Riccio reads: "Old love has put forth a shoot, or at least a bud."

255. 1546. Madrigal. For Vittoria Colonna? Earlier versions go back to 1535–40.

256. By 1545–46. Madrigal.

257. Date uncertain. 1546–47? Unfinished sonnet. Perhaps for Vittoria Colonna.

258. By 1546. Madrigal. Perhaps for Vittoria Colonna, as commentators have suggested. The tone, however, is more like that of poems to the lady beautiful and cruel.

259. After 1546. Sonnet. A first draft, several times revised, seems to go back to 1546. Early versions were addressed to *signor mio*, probably Cavalieri.

260. After 1546–47. Sonnet. For Cavalieri, according to Girardi.

261. 1546. Sonnet. Possibly for Vittoria Colonna.

262. Shortly before 1547, with a version dating from 1534. Madrigal. Barelli has commented that the many drafts are "much tormented."

263. 1547. Madrigal. Tierce, Nones and Vespers are the canonical hours for morning, afternoon and evening.

264. 1547. Madrigal. Authorities are divided as to whether the soul (*l'alma*) of line 4 refers to the poet's or the lady's. She is probably Vittoria Colonna.

265. 1547. Madrigal. For Vittoria Colonna, who died on February 25.

266. 1547. Sonnet. On the death of Vittoria Colonna. Michelangelo was then seventy-two years old.

267. 1546–49. *Capitolo, terza rima.* This piece was marked for publication and therefore seems to have existed in one version by 1546. The reference to his kidney trouble in line 36 suggests a date of 1548–49. Arachne of line 5 was a girl so proficient at weaving that Athena, jealous, turned her into a spider.

268. 1547. Unfinished madrigal, written after Vittoria Colonna died.

269. 1547. Madrigal. Penned across a pencil sketch for the *Last Judgment.*

270. Ca. 1547. Fragment. Some have placed it after the death of Vittoria Colonna in February 1547.

271. 1547 or soon after. Unfinished sonnet. We can only guess what the ending was going to say.

272. 1547. Sonnet. On the death of Vittoria Colonna. The "kindlier arrows" of line 13 are the ones that remind the poet of divine, rather than earthly, love.

273. 1547. Unfinished sonnet.

274. 1547. Sonnet. Line 4 refers to the soul's preexistence with God.

275. 1547–50. Is a statue the speaker in this obscure fragment? Michelangelo, then working on St. Peter's, was spending much time among great slabs of rock from the stone quarries.

276. 1547–50. Sonnet.

277. April–May 1550. Sonnet. Dedicated to Giorgio Vasari, in appreciation of his "Life of Michelangelo Buonarroti" in the first edition of *Lives of the Artists* (1550). In the next edition (1568), Vasari included the sonnet.

278. Late, date uncertain. Contrary meanings have been found in these proverb-like lines, depending on whether one takes the leaves to stand for luxuriousness or fruitlessness.

279. Late, date uncertain. The octave of a sonnet, though the sense is complete in itself?

280. Late, date uncertain. Octave of a sonnet?

281. Ca. 1552. Unfinished sonnet.

282. Late, date uncertain. The lack of rhyme suggests that these lines are intended as one of the two tercets of a sonnet, the rhymes to be completed in the missing tercet.

283. 1552. Probably the two tercets of a sonnet, although lines 2 and 5 do not have the expected rhyme.

284. 1552. Sestet of an unfinished sonnet.

285. 1552–54. Sonnet. There are many versions of this poem. On September 19, 1554, Michelangelo—then seventy-nine—sent it to Vasari with a letter that begins: "You'll probably say that I'm old and out of my mind, wanting to write sonnets. But since many say I'm in my second childhood, I might as well act the part."

286. Ca. 1552–54. Unfinished sonnet.

287. Ca. 1552–54. Perhaps the beginning of a sonnet, although the quatrain is complete in itself.

288. 1555. Sonnet. Michelangelo sent a copy of this and the following sonnet to Vasari with a letter: "I'm sending you two sonnets; though they're not much *[cosa sciocca]*. I'm doing it so you can see where my thoughts are. And when you're eighty-one, as I am, I think you'll believe me."

289. 1555. Numerous drafts. In the *Last Judgment* "faith's chain" is illustrated by the rosary beads, with which a husky angel is hauling two grateful souls up toward God. A central idea of the Catholic reform movement, of which Vittoria Colonna was a prominent member, was that salvation was to be attained not by good works, but by faith alone (Luther's *fide sola*). De Tolnay (108) thinks that Michelangelo illustrates this by having the blessed souls rising with supernatural help (their faith), and the damned, however vigorous, falling because they rely on their own strength. In the *Conversion of St. Paul* "Michelangelo illustrated the overwhelming force of the grace of God in the shaft of light falling from the abruptly foreshortened aerial figure of God toward the powerful but now blinded and prostrate figure of Saul

. . ." (Bull, 312). Loren Partridge (58–59) has claimed that the resurrecting souls (bottom left) display two distinct types: the larger, energetic group, far left, are making a determined effort to rise; those to the right, lying prostrate, need the help of angels, who have already hoisted two of them into the air. The two groups symbolize salvation through personal responsi- bility, as shown in good works performed, and salvation by divine grace alone. The prominence given the martyrs in the fresco also "forcefully re- futes the doctrine of judgment by faith alone" (84).

290. 1555 or later. Sonnet. See in the *Last Judgment* Christ's "long arm, hovering," as in line 11. This poem and 294 were published in Venice soon after Michelangelo's death in an anthology of "noble Tuscan poets."

291–92. 1555 or later. Unfinished sonnets.

293. 1555 or later. Sonnet.

294–95. After 1555. Sonnets.

296. Probably 1555. Sonnet. Many versions exist.

297. Ca. 1555. Quatrain.

298. Late, date uncertain. Sonnet. Clements believes that this poem, which mentions in line 3 *gli spirti eletti* (the chosen spirits) was not merely suggested by Vittoria Colonna's sonnet, beginning *gli angeli eletti* (the chosen angels), but "constitutes a clear case of plagiarism on his part" (Clements, 330). In the two poems only lines 9–11 (or part of them) are alike. Colonna's lines would translate as

The sun hid its glittering tresses;

bedrock shattered; the mountains gaped;

earth trembled; the waters became turbulent.

Since such details are available in many sources (including Dante), from the Bible on, and since the two sonnets have little else but some rhyming words in common, there seems no need to invoke "plagiarism" here. Colonna's poem may well have been in Michelangelo's mind when he wrote his own, but his theme is developed in a wholly different, and far richer, way.

299. 1555–59. The sonnet is a thank you, perhaps to Vasari, for the gifts mentioned. St. Michael is often depicted holding the scales with which he weighs the merits of the souls after death. The boat imagery in lines 5–8 may suggest that Michelangelo considered himself fairly swamped with favors and is lolling in the kindness of others.

300. 1556. Sonnet. In reply to a letter from his friend the Archbishop Ludovic Beccadelli (the Monsignor, line 2), who was about to be transferred to distant Dalmatia. Michelangelo's long-time servant and companion, called "Urbino" (line 10), had died the year before.

301. 1560. The first eight lines of a sonnet? The poem is similar to a letter of the same year, "perhaps the most poignant of the entire correspon- dence, [which] marks the end of a career" (Clements, 294). As the poem admits to moral failings, the letter admits to professional failings: "I may perhaps be easily deceived by self-interest and old age and, contrary to my intention, as a result have caused damage and loss [to St. Peter's]." Michel- angelo asks (in vain) to be relieved of his authority over the project.

302. 1560. Michelangelo's last known poem, an unfinished sonnet, written when he was eighty-five years old.

Bibliography

TEXTS

Barelli, Ettore, ed. *Michelangelo: Rime.* With an introduction by Giovanni Testori. Milan: Biblioteca Universale Rizzoli, 1975; 4th ed., 1990.

Mastrocola, Paola, ed. *Rime e Lettere di Michelangelo.* Torino: Classici UTET. Unione Tipografico-Editrice Torinese, 1992.

BACKGROUND

Bull, George. *Michelangelo: A Biography.* New York: St. Martin's Press, 1995.

Cambon, Glauco. *Michelangelo's Poetry: Fury of Form.* Princeton: Princeton University Press, 1985.

Clements, Robert J. *The Poetry of Michelangelo.* New York: New York University Press, 1965.

Condivi, Ascanio. "Life of Michelangelo Buonarroti," in *Michelangelo: Life, Letters, and Poetry.* Trans. George Bull. Oxford and New York: Oxford University Press, 1987.

de Tolnay, Charles. *Michelangelo: Sculptor, Painter, Architect.* Princeton: Princeton University Press, 1975.

Montale, Eugenio. *Michelangelo Poeta.* With an introduction by Armando Brissoni. Bologna: Massimilano Boni Editore, 1976.

Partridge, Loren, Fabrizio Mancinelli and Gianluigi Colalucci. *The Last Judgment: A Glorious Restoration.* New York: Harry N. Abrams, 1997.

Ramsden, E. H., trans. and ed. *The Letters of Michelangelo.* Stanford: Stanford University Press, 1963.

Saslow, James M. trans. and annot. *The Poetry of Michelangelo.* New Haven: Yale University Press, 1991.

Vasari, Giorgio. "The Life of Michelangelo Buonarroti," in *Lives of the Artists* I. Trans. George Bull. Harmondsworth: Penguin Books, 1987.

Vecchi, Pierluigi de, ed. *The Sistine Chapel: A Glorious Restoration.* New York: Harry N. Abrams, 1994.